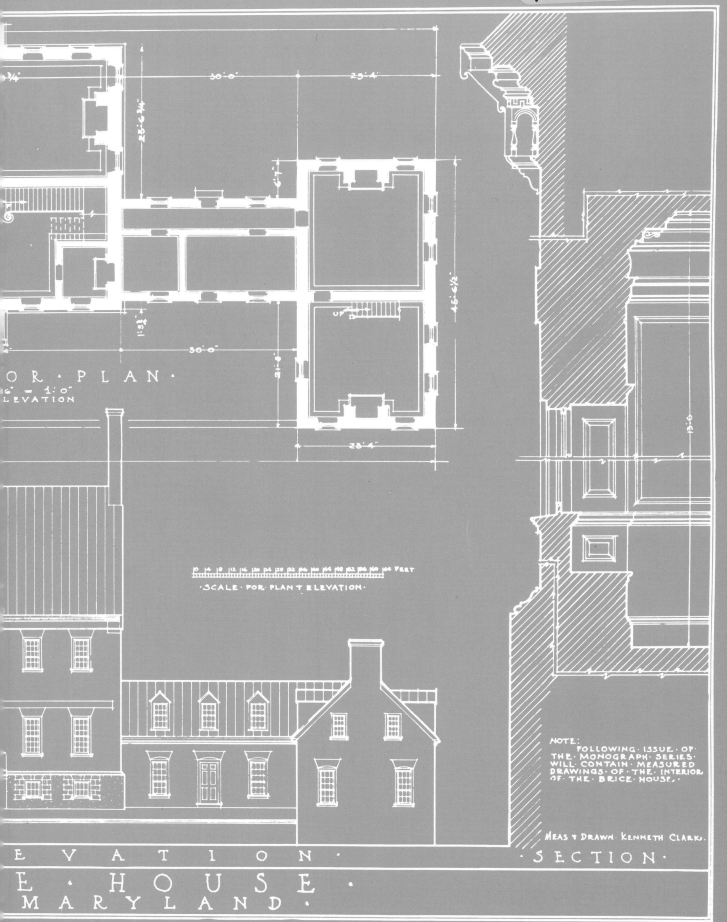

OR · PLAN ·
LEVATION

SCALE · FOR · PLAN + ELEVATION ·

0 4 8 12 16 20 24 28 32 36 40 44 48 52 56 60 FEET

NOTE:
FOLLOWING · ISSUE · OF ·
THE · MONOGRAPH · SERIES ·
WILL · CONTAIN · MEASURED ·
DRAWINGS · OF · THE · INTERIOR ·
OF · THE · BRICE · HOUSE ·

MEAS ₹ DRAWN · KENNETH CLARK.

· SECTION ·

E V A T I O N ·

E · H O U S E ·

M A R Y L A N D ·

VILLAGE ARCHITECTURE
OF EARLY NEW ENGLAND

Architectural Treasures of Early America

VILLAGE ARCHITECTURE OF EARLY NEW ENGLAND

From material originally published as
The White Pine Series of Architectural Monographs
edited by
Russell F. Whitehead and Frank Chouteau Brown

Lisa C. Mullins, Editor

Roy Underhill, Consultant

A Publication of
THE NATIONAL HISTORICAL SOCIETY

Library of Congress Cataloging-in-Publication Data

Village architecture of early New England.
    (Architectural treasures of Early America; 7)
    1. Architecture—New England. 2. Architecture, Colonial—New England. 3. Outbuildings—New England.
4. Fences—New England. I. Mullins, Lisa C.
II. Underhill, Roy. III. Series: Architectural treasures of Early America (Harrisburg, Pa.); 7.
NA715.V5   1988   720'.974   87-14109
ISBN 0-918678-26-9

The original photographs reproduced in this publication are from the collection of drawings and photographs in "The White Pine Monograph Series, Collected and Edited by Russell F. Whitehead, The George P. Lindsay Collection." The collection, part of the research and reference collections of The American Institute of Architects, Washington, D.C., was acquired by the Institute in 1955 from the Whitehead estate, through the cooperation of Mrs. Russell F. Whitehead, and the generosity of the Weyerhauser Timber Company, which purchased the collection for presentation to the Institute. The research and reference collections of the Institute are available for public use. A written request for such use is required so that space may be reserved and assistance made available.

CONTENTS

THE NEW ENGLAND CHARACTER

Thoughts of the New England Town often yield one of two conflicting images. One is that of Puritan intolerance; of people obsessed, as H. L. Mencken claimed, with the idea that "somewhere, someone might be having a good time." The other, is that of the Town Meeting, joy in freedom and the grassroots of democracy. Both images are part of the New England character as we see it today: Sure competence intersown with wry wit, raised with devotion from stony ground.

What about this repressive reputation? Why, for example, in 1631, was Governor Winthrop so displeased with Thomas Dudley's new house in Cambridge? Winthrop criticized Dudley, his Deputy Governor, for bestowing "such cost about wainscotting and adorning his house." Apparently this wainscotting amounted to some clapboards nailed around the walls, but Dudley was compelled to defend himself. He claimed that the wainscot paneling was only for warmth, implying that, otherwise, he took no pleasure in it at all.

Winthrop sounds like the classic pill, but his concerns were more practical than puritanical. He felt that public officials had to set a good example for their lessers and could not afford even simple luxuries. Harmonious relations had to be enforced in this new and dangerous land. The Puritan leaders did believe in one type of personal freedom. They plainly stated that all who would disagree with their doctrine "shall have free liberty to keep away from us."

Practicality and common sense are primary virtues of the New Englander, and the lack of these are prime sources of amusement. Like a woodpile of crooked branches (so crooked that you could chase a cat through it from any point on the compass), these tales have been collected in *A Treasury of New England Folklore* edited by B. A. Botkin (New York: Crown Publishers, 1957).

These old stories from the *Treasury* have been renovated and reworked to serve each new generation. For example, one village innkeeper told her summer guests that a rocking chair in the front room had been the favorite of George Washington. The guests were unable to resist secretly carving slivers of wood from the chair to take for souvenirs. Within a month the chair was so thoroughly distressed that she could sell it as an antique for thrice its cost when new. She went through a half dozen chairs every season.

Some people were not satisfied with small chips of wood. One wealthy resident of Cape Cod decided that her estate needed a Dutch windmill. She found one in Falmouth, bought it, and had it moved back to her estate in Chatham. Soon thereafter, an old-timer in the village stopped by. "Well, well," he exclaimed, "I'm glad to see Jim Eldrege's old mill back in Chatham. You know, a man from Falmouth came here fifteen or twenty years ago and took it away. Sort of wanted to decorate his grounds."

Another source of wit are the trials of the environment. This is the stony land best suited to raising men—some places with ten months of winter and two months of hard sledding—where stone walls must be built lying flat so that they will stand upright when the wind blows them over. One group of men were nailing shingles on the roof of the church when the fog rolled in. They kept on working until the shingles ran out. Only when they climbed down to fetch another load did they discover that they had shingled twenty feet out onto the fog.

But just as these stories grow and change form, so has the serious analysis of the roles of culture and the environment in shaping American building. Many of the houses featured in this volume are also found in the enlightening book, *The Framed Houses of Massachusetts Bay, 1625-1725* by Abbott Lowell Cummings (Cambridge: Harvard University Press, 1979). *Framed Houses* embodies the latest scholarship in architectural history and is an invaluable companion to this volume.

In *Framed Houses,* you may see how Swans Hall in Suffolk, England, the original home of Abraham Browne, relates to the home he built in 1633 in Watertown, Massachusetts (shown in Chapter 5 of this volume). Many of the houses originally examined in the *White Pine Series of Architectural Monographs* have been repaired or restored over the years, revealing new details of their construction. *Framed Houses* will show you the hidden structure of the Cooper-Austin House of Cambridge, the Tristam Coffin House of Newbury, and the Turner House of Salem. A photograph in *Framed Houses* of the Turner House, the "House of the Seven Gables," taken before the 1910 restoration is particularly revealing when compared with the post-restoration version shown in Chapter 2 of this volume.

Salem, Watertown, Cambridge; these towns are probably familiar names to you, but the subject of Chapter 1 may not be. The unspoiled village of Stotham will be difficult to find on your map. Stotham is a charming place to visit, even though you may well discover, "you can't get there from here."

ROY UNDERHILL
MASTER HOUSEWRIGHT
COLONIAL WILLIAMSBURG

AND WHY CAN'T YOU GET THERE FROM HERE?

"Every picture tells a story." How often have we heard this aphorism? In the case of Chapter 1, this statement is especially pertinent. Stotham, a "typical and unspoiled village", is a place that exists only in the mind of the author Hubert Ripley. The first chapter in this volume suggests that there is no defense when a sly editor and an imaginative and talented storyteller set out to hoodwink their audience.

The plot began innocently enough. In 1920 Russell Whitehead, the editor of the *White Pine Series of Architectural Monographs,* and Hubert Ripley, a prominent architect and writer, were examining a drawer full of unused photographs that had been eliminated from various monographs because of space constraints. The two lamented the fact that such wonderful photographs were going to waste. Both agreed that the public should not be deprived of seeing these important architectural sites. After careful thought, they decided to use the photographs to illustrate a monograph on a fictitious New England village that Ripley would create. And so a "typical example, although, perhaps, not so well known, of the unspoiled New England Village" was born.

For years no one questioned the authenticity of the Stotham village and the whole story was accepted at face value by thousands of architects who received the monograph. The plot unraveled after Leicester B. Holland, the former head of the Fine Arts Department of the Library of Congress, cornered Whitehead and asked for his assistance in identifying sites in the April 1920 monograph that Leicester was having trouble finding. Only then was Whitehead forced to reveal the hoax.

Even today, many architects famiar with the series did not know about the hoax. For the edification of our readers, here are the true identifications of the buildings featured in Chapter 1:

Page	*As Listed*	*True Identity*
10	Jenks-Greenleaf House	Unidentified
12 (upper)	Unidentified	Unidentified
12 (lower)	Nahum Bodkins House	Unidentified
13 (upper)	Unidentified	Unidentified
13 (lower)	House on Sandy Point	Joseph Lynde House, Melrose, Massachusetts
14	Cadwallader Simpkins House	Aspinwall House, Brookline, Massachusetts
15 (upper)	Balustrade of Rogers House	Unidentified
15 (lower)	Salmon White House	Abram Mitchell House, Chester, Connecticut
16	Salmon White House	Abram Mitchell House, Chester, Connecticut
17	Podbury-Ives House	House in Bedford, Massachusetts
18	Podbury-Ives House	House in Bedford, Massachusetts
19	Heman Billings House	Champion House, East Haddam, Connecticut
20 (upper)	Uriel Underwood House	Wheeler House, Oxford, New Hampshire
20 (lower)	Lemuel Short House	Unidentified
21	Obadiah Witherspoon House	Unidentified
22	First Meeting House of Stotham Congregational Society	North Woodbury Congregational Church, Woodbury, Connecticut

A New England Village

Text by
Hubert G. Ripley
Originally published in 1920 as White Pine Monograph
Volume VI, Number 2

Detail of Doorway
JENKS-GREENLEAF HOUSE

A NEW ENGLAND VILLAGE

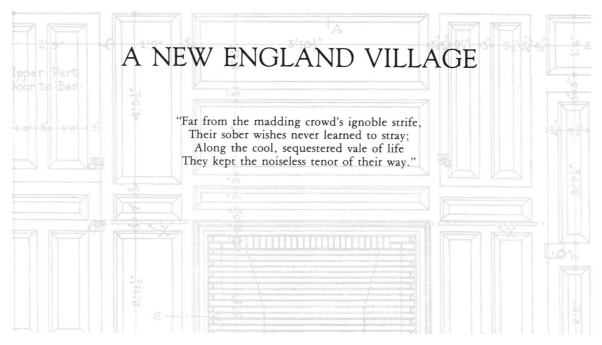

"Far from the madding crowd's ignoble strife,
Their sober wishes never learned to stray;
Along the cool, sequestered vale of life
They kept the noiseless tenor of their way."

WHEN Zabdiel Podbury fled from Stoke-on-Tritham in the spring of 1689 with Drusilla Ives, taking passage on the bark *Promise*, sailing for Massachusetts Bay, it was not realized at the time that, from this union, and the joint labors of the Penthesilean pair, the village of Stotham (so named by them in memory of their autochthonous abode) would in later days come to be regarded as a typical example, although, perhaps, not so well known, of the unspoiled New England Village.

The terms typical and unspoiled are used advisedly, as a reference to the illustrations will show. There are, possibly, no especially striking or far-famed structures, no wealth of fine carving or ornamental detail, no grand estates or mansion houses, yet from its early simplicity, and quality of chaste primness, the village has slowly developed, until, as it now stands, a characteristic chapter of New England endeavor lies spread out on the gently undulating plain, lapped by the salt waters of the inland cove on one side, and stretching out by the fertile meadows of the river on the other. The first temporary houses soon gave way to more permanent structures, and the tradition of restrained, conservative building has been faithfully followed even to the present day.

Fortunately there was no occasion, and, what is more unusual, no inclination to depart from the customs and practices of the earlier settlers, in buildings of a later period, and the blighting hand of the real estate promoter, and the withering touch of the speculative builder, are conspicuously lacking.

To the Podbury family—who may well be termed the founders of Stotham—eleven children were born, seven boys and four girls. Adoniram, who married Hephzibah Jenks, died in his early thirties, and the descendants of his widow, who afterwards married Theron Greenleaf, still keep up the old Jenks-Greenleaf House, the doorway of which is shown in the frontispiece.

Ira Podbury married Serena Bellows, and their son Manasseh, afterwards a colonel in the Stotham Fusileers, who made an enviable record in the Revolutionary War (*q.v.* Bilks' *History of the Early Revolutionary Volunteer Guards Associations* and Cranitche's *Curious Antiquities of New England Villages*, pp. 329–427 *et seq.*), the financier of the family, built the second Podbury-Ives House, which was the pride of the village.

Obadiah and Nahum Podbury died in their early youth, Elnathan was lost at sea, but the youngest son, Obijah, early developing a natural instinct and taste for building, constructed, with the assistance of three others of the first settlers, many of the simple old farmhouses, a few examples of which are illustrated in the following pages.

Of the four daughters, Keturah, Mehitabel, Evelina and Zoë, nothing is known, except of the youngest. Zoë married Heman Billings, and the Billings House, designed by Speat, a Scotch architect, with its sloping gardens, gently terracing down to the river, has been kept in almost per-

The only farmhouse in Stotham concerning which
the records show lack of authentic data.

the salt marsh meadows was just starting at the time, and the firm of Simpkins and Plainfield, which had prospered since its inception, undertook to finance the tannery business, and started a shoe and harness shop in a small way as a sideline. From the very beginning the venture prospered, and the tannery grew and the shop expanded into the old stone factory, with its easily obtainable water power from a natural dam, slightly enlarged and extended by building a mill race, running close by old Obed Stowe's place.

Ebenezer was astute enough to retain control of the business, while duly sensible of the help he was receiving from the proprietors of the general store, and in the course of time amassed a considerable sum of money for those days. He was a generous contributor to the Congregational church — not the one shown in our illustration, but an earlier type, on whose sturdy foundations of rubble the new church now stands. Barzillai Plainfield retired from business while still in the hale and hearty forties, and

fect condition, altered but slightly and with reverent care, as evidences of the relentless tooth of time began to show here and there, until even now its pristine charm is but rounded and enhanced, mellowed and softened, forming a part of a well-nigh perfect example of simple domesticity and dignified unity of fitness of structure to the enframing landscape.

Generations of blushing maidens have swung on the old Billings gate, opening on the path leading to the meadows, in the pale light of the harvest moon, lending shy ear to the rustic swains of the village, as in whispered and halting phrases they spoke of their hopes and aspirations; and as a result of these meetings, old traditions were kept alive, and more and more houses were built and hearthstones kept bright, sanded floors neatly traced in swerving lines, and the simple life of the early settlers passed on through the mellowing influences of time.

Cadwallader Simpkins came to Stotham in 1734 in company with Barzillai Plainfield and opened a general store. Ebenezer Rogers' tannery down on

The house which Obijah Podbury built for his
stepbrother Nahum Bodkins.

built an almost palatial mansion, for its simple surroundings, yet the details are well contained and the ornament sparingly applied.

There is a curious story, too long to be related here (for complete details consult Cranitche's *Antiquities*, Vol. XIX, from which sterling work many of the facts here related were drawn), concerning the Rogers mansion, better known under its local title, as the Haunted House, or the House of Buried Treasure. Briefly, its outline is as follows:

Ichabod Somes, a wild, untamed, red-headed youth of the village, ran away at the age of sixteen, and shipped before the mast on the privateer *Polly*, at the beginning of the French and Indian Wars. Ichabod appears to have been a strapping youth, tall, and well formed for his age and of callipygian aspect. In later years it used to be said by the few who were fortunate, or unfortunate, enough to have encountered him, that his single remaining eye, the other having been lost in one of his numerous encounters with Barbary pirates, possessed a

This house was entirely constructed of material cut on the spot.

peculiar basilisk quality before which even the stoutest heart quailed, and the most resolute spirit became as weak as babbling waters.

After many and various adventures, enduring through a period of some ten or a dozen years, during which time Ichabod had, by sheer force of dominance, attained command of a vessel of his own, all trace of him became lost.

Meanwhile the Rogers mansion suffered many vicissitudes. An old darkey servant, named Phinehas Moseley, was discovered one frosty December morning on the floor of the woodshed, with his throat cut from ear to ear. It happened that the family were away at the time, and the crime would not have been discovered so shortly after its committal, had not Gershom Judkins, Obijah Podbury's foreman and right-hand man, happened to be passing by, and, as it was a cold morning, knowing that the Rogers family were away, decided to step in for the wicker demijohn of Santa Cruz rum that old Phinehas had drawn off from the Rogers rum barrel, a little at a time, so that the gradual

Old farmhouse on Sandy Point, built by Obijah Podbury.

lowering of its contents would not be noted by the family. Appalled by the sight that met his eyes as he entered the woodshed, he dashed out with a cry on his lips, only to be intercepted by a tall bearded stranger, with a single piercing eye, who neatly and deftly knocked him down with a staggering blow from the butt of his derringer.

These details were only learned little by little at a later period, for, when discovered, foreman Judkins was picked up for dead, and never com-

leading from the wine cellar, where the rum barrel stood, to the outbuildings, furnished a ready means of access and escape to one familiar with the secret of the house and grounds, as Somes undoubtedly was), mainly from the fact that a large heavy derringer, marked with a skull and cross-bones, intertwined with the initials "I. S." (now under a glass and mahogany case in the rooms of the Stotham Historical Society in the basement of the Town

CADWALLADER SIMPKINS HOUSE

The large shagbark in the front yard was planted at
the time of the raising of the frame of the house.

pletely recovered from the effects of the terrible blow.

The Rogers house was found to be intact, except for the loss of some valuable papers, in particular the deeds and description of the Rogers title to certain meadow lands, some overseas securities in the Dutch East India Company, and a considerable amount in pieces of eight, that were known to have been locked up behind a secret panel in the dining room wainscoting.

Somes, who by now had acquired a very unsavory reputation, through reports that had trickled into Stotham from time to time, whether rightly or wrongly, was always popularly considered to have committed the crime (a tunnel

Hall), was picked up in the back yard near the woodshed.

Strangely enough, Rogers and his wife never returned to Stotham. All trace of them was lost, and the house was closed for years. After a time it came to be called the Haunted House, and was shunned and avoided by all.

Later generations forgot the qualms and fears of their forebears, and, in spite of its atrabilarious appearance, became quite proud and boastful of its notoriety. Many strangers wandered out through the daggle of the front yard on sunny May afternoons, poking around here and there, first under the marble tiles of the piazza (which came over in ballast in the Peruvian bark

Calisaya from Demerara), and afterwards through the main rooms and closets, seeking whatever might be found of interest, in the hope of discovering some trace of the Rogers property, or some clew left by the assailants of Phinehas Moseley.

Thus the old Rogers house gradually disappeared, melting away slowly, baluster by baluster, and door by door, until the historical society finally claimed the poor scarred remains for its own, and, for the last thirteen years, has kept the vestiges of the departed grandeur and the boast of Stotham from the despoiling touch of the vandal.

A very beautiful and quaintly carved pine mantel from the Rogers front parlor has been set up in the room of the society, together with a console from the dining

DETAIL OF BALUSTRADE FROM PORTICO OF THE ROGERS MANSION

The original baluster, from which these were copied, is said to have been brought from Baltimore.

room door frame, carved out of a solid white-pine plank, three and three-quarters inches thick and thirty inches long, portraying the birth of Ariadne. It was rescued in almost perfect condition, and still retains all its pristine freshness without a crack or flaw. The cornice of the porch, some of the columns, and a few of the balusters may also be seen.

In detail the balusters over the front porch show touches of Southern influence, and it is said they were copied from a pattern brought home by Ebenezer Rogers, who traveled often to Baltimore, where he had many business and social connections, while still active in the affairs of the tannery.

Main Street winds gently up-hill from the village square, lined with stately elms and locusts.

SALMON WHITE HOUSE ON MAIN STREET

The clapboards were originally painted a deep saffron, but this has lately been changed and the effectiveness of the house somewhat diminished in consequence.

Detail of Main Façade
SALMON WHITE HOUSE
The spider-web window in the second story is from sketches by Robert Adam.

Front Door Detail
PODBURY-IVES HOUSE
Note that the wide necking of the pilasters is not at all inharmonious in combination with the frieze and architrave above.
Ruben Duren, Architect

On each side are the principal residences of Stotham's prominent citizens. The Beriah Matthews House, now owned by two very charming maiden ladies, who still serve steaming, fragrant Bohea in fragile Chelsea, with crisp buttered Cassava biscuits fresh from a hot trivet in the east parlor, at four-thirty precisely each afternoon, is quite as interesting in its interior as the promise of its exterior indicates.

To one who has enjoyed the privilege of assisting on those occasions, it is a pleasure rarely

amassed a fortune in the East India trade, and the east dining room is still the most perfect example of Chinese Chippendale extant in New England). It is also true to a lesser degree of Gideon Pond's house and the slightly older Joab Hubbard House. Salmon White's house, sometimes called the Crocus House, on account of the peculiar shade of saffron originally used on the sidings, had a somewhat quaint origin: the main facts, of which the following is only the briefest abstract, were obtained from a pamphlet

PODBURY-IVES HOUSE
Forms a chaste silhouette on the heights overlooking the river.
Ruben Duren, Architect

to be experienced elsewhere, to hear and listen to their delightful conversation, to follow the reminiscences so quaintly worded, and to experience the gentle glow of their charming hospitality.

It is the personal contact with the people themselves that lends an elusive charm to the externals of their environment. As the houses seem to show by their aspect, they are the personification, in their external and internal attributes, of the simplicity of life, and the friendly point of view, of the gentle folk who live in them.

This is true of the Silas Mann House, now occupied by his great-grandchildren (Silas Mann

on the shelves of the historical society, entitled "A Short Account of the Experiences of Salmon White on the Sailing Vessel *Roxanne* from Stotham Narrows to Lucca, Anno Domini MDCCXCIX," published by Asher Harrison, 12½ Main Street, Stotham, June, 1823.

At the age of thirty-seven Salmon White, at that time just recovering from an attack of enteric anaemia, shipped as supercargo on the brigantine *Roxanne* in ballast for Lucca. After a passage of one hundred and nineteen days, during which head winds and cross currents were encountered, and many hair-breadth escapes from the dangers of the deep, all faithfully set forth in the log of Captain Eldad Bottomly, the island of Teneriffe was raised, four points sou'-sou'-west by west off the larboard bow, on the morning of October 23. Dropping anchor in the harbor of Risotto, at the base of the famous peak of Teneriffe, at that time possessing an unenviable notoriety as the haunt of buccaneers of the Spanish Main, it was learned that a young Scotchman by the name of Robert Adam was extremely anxious to leave the island at the earliest possible moment, as well he

to erect a newer and more appropriate house for a man of his circumstances and constantly growing family, whiled away the long hours of the dog-watch by making rough sketches for his new friend, showing, in more or less detail, the inspiration that pervades the southeast façade of Salmon White's house, the peculiar arrangement of the staircase, and more especially the mouldings around the inside of the main door framing.

Some of these sketches may now be seen on the walls of the historical society, and a close

Southwesterly View
HEMAN BILLINGS HOUSE
Note the quality of line given to the façade by the modulation of the siding.

might be, having been marooned there when all, save he, went down in the wreck of the *Bouncing Betty*.

Young Adam and the supercargo soon struck up a warm friendship, due partly to a natural sympathy in ideals, and cemented permanently by the happy faculty which White possessed in the mixing of Santa Cruz sours, a beverage that young Adam declared topped his favorite negus by several pegs. After a few slugs of this delectable stingo had been brought to a perfect blend with the swizzle-stick, wielded by the deft fingers of a master of the craft, Adam, learning that White, on his return to Stotham, intended

scrutiny reveals the initials "R. A.," faintly traced in sanded ink, on the lower right-hand side of some scraps of paper, evidently torn from the ship's log, on which they were made.

In particular, the spider-web window which adorns the main façade, shows the influence of Adam, though its execution lacks finesse, and may be said to have an original quaintness on that account, not always observed in the works of the famous brothers who afterwards became the vogue, and developed to a high degree of delicacy the more sturdy forms of their predecessors.

Space will not permit mention of all that is of interest in Stotham, fascinating as even the most

URIEL UNDERWOOD'S HOUSE FROM THE RIVER

The proportion and balance between the outbuildings and the main house is particularly good.

LEMUEL SHORT HOUSE

Now occupied by his great-grandnephew.

casual study of its history may be, but some of the more prominent structures must not be allowed to pass without a note here and there, to call attention to certain of their characteristics.

Obadiah Witherspoon's house at the head of the village green, now owned by Miss Sophronia Winterbottom, a grandniece of Obadiah's, where she takes in a few paying guests for the summer months, is the proud possessor of a portico worthy of the most careful study.

The details of the Ionic capitals and the mod-

a façade of great restraint and dignity and at the same time a purity of outline and sense of proportion rarely excelled by buildings of that date.

Uriel Underwood's house, a view of which is shown from the meadows leading to the river, has a nice balance and relation of outbuildings to main structures that is worthy of careful analysis.

Consciously or unconsciously, the earlier generations of New England settlers seemed to

OBADIAH WITHERSPOON HOUSE ON CENTRE STREET
Note the perfect preservation of the Ionic capitals,
carved from solid blocks of clear white pine.

ulation of the entablature have all been most faithfully and studiously wrought with reverent care, the capitals being hewn by hand out of solid blocks of the finest white pine, and, protected by frequent applications of pure white lead and Calcutta oil, they are as perfect and fresh as the day they left Lemuel Short's shop down by the old dam.

The house of old Joab Drinkwater, who married Corinna Kane in his sixty-ninth year, Corinna being then a mere slip of a girl, dazzled by the worldly possessions of the redoubtable Major of the one-time Stotham Fusileers, shows

strike just the right note of proportion, harmony, fitness, and, what is more impressive, the distinctive character of their lives in the design of their buildings. Even a glance at the exterior of their houses and the most casual study of the planning and material from which they were built, leads to the inevitable conclusion that here, at least, exists an indigenous architecture wholly suited to its purposes.

Almost more than in any other village, this quality is to be noted in Stotham, where the quintessence of naturalness finds its ultimate expression.

FIRST MEETING HOUSE OF THE STOTHAM CONGREGATIONAL SOCIETY
Built on the foundations of an earlier church. The detail of the entablature and
the modulation of the pilasters are more refined than those of the first church.

Salem, Massachusetts

Text by
Frank Chouteau Brown
Photographs by
Arthur C. Haskell
Originally published in 1937 as White Pine Monograph
Volume XXIII, Number 2

PINGREE HOUSE—1810—ESSEX STREET, SALEM, MASSACHUSETTS
Samuel McIntire, Architect

SALEM, MASSACHUSETTS

AS we have already seen, Salem was the first town to be settled within the district covered by the Charter given to the members of the Massachusetts Bay Company by King Charles the First. Nevertheless, upon the arrival of the first group of settlers engaged under this Charter, who had been forwarded from England by the Governor and members of the company, under the command of Captain John Endecott, they found Mr. Roger Conant, and several others, already established in residence upon the land sloping down to Salem Harbor.

When Edward Winslow went back to England from the Plymouth Colony in 1623–1624, he secured from Lord Sheffield a charter to "fish, fowle, hawke, truck, and trade" on "Cape Anne," and immediately on his return to Plymouth on the *Charity*, in March of 1624, the ship was reladen with material and some Plymouth men and sailed to set up the "Great House," the frame of which had been prepared in England, along with the required fishing "stages," and begin the fishing and trading venture on Cape Ann.

This did not prove very successful, and Roger Conant, who was then at Nantasket, was asked to go to the Cape and take charge, in the interest of the Dorchester Company. This was late in 1624. In 1625 the Dorchester Company dissolved; but, encouraged by letters from Rev. John White of Dorchester, England, Roger Conant and a few followers withdrew to a "fruitful neck of land in Naumkeag," where setting up their houses and planting land crops, they waited for the promised reenforcements, which finally arrived under Capt. John Endecott, in June of 1628, supplanting Roger Conant. But on June 12, 1630, Endecott was supplanted in turn by the arrival of Gov. John Winthrop, in the *Arbella*, which was the first of four vessels which had sailed from the Isle of Wight, on April 8; the others being the *Jewell*, arriving June 13; the *Ambrose*, arriving June 18; and the *Talbot*, on July 2. Governor Winthrop was accompanied by Sir Richard Saltonstall, Lt.-Gov. Thomas Dudley, Rev. George Phillips, and a number of others.

Meanwhile, Endecott had the "fayre dwelling" on Cape Ann "shook" and brought down to Naumkeag (now renamed Salem in honor of the peaceful arrangement arrived at between the "Old Planters" and the New) and reassembled again upon the westerly part of his lot, which lay between Washington, Federal, and St. Peter's streets, facing Washington Street. By this arrangement the "Old Planters" were given house lots together along the line of the present Essex Street.

The Rev. Francis Higginson, who arrived with about two hundred settlers in June of 1629, speaks of a "faire house newly built for the Governor," elsewhere also described as "of the model in England first called Tudor, and afterwards the Elizabethan," and as having two stories with a sharp pitched roof.

Endecott removed to Boston in 1665, and died in 1666, his wife following him about 1678, and his house had entirely disappeared in 1684. In 1682, part of the Endecott property was sold to Benjamin Hooper, who built upon it a single-room house, two stories high; which structure is undoubtedly the southeasterly portion of the present Hathaway House, which was removed in 1911 to the grounds beside the John Turner House (House of the Seven Gables, on Turner Street, overlooking the Harbor). The *only* uncertainty is as to whether or not Benjamin Hooper incorporated the Gov. Endecott dwelling into the new house he was building in 1682! If that *was* done, the portion of the Hathaway House mentioned would go back to 1624, and probably to the West of England for its origin — and so would be the oldest house frame existing in this country! The elaborate design of one of the posts is shown in the detail sketch. It is unlike any other post remaining in New England and has the peculiarly mellow yellow tone of old English oak. Miss Emmerton treats very fairly of the history of this and the adjoining houses in her book, *The Chronicles of Three Old Houses*. As to the importation of the frame from England, early records of other trading settlements (even that of Charlton — now Charlestown — nearby) indicate it was quite customary to send out the frame of a large house — usually called the Great

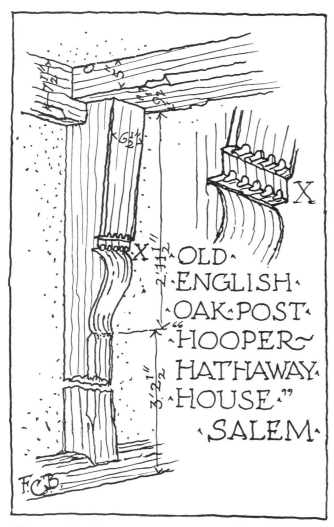

·OLD· ·ENGLISH· ·OAK·POST· "HOOPER~ HATHAWAY· ·HOUSE·" ·SALEM·

mouldings" along both edges, covering the timbered frame, which was nogged with brick laid up in clay, and daubed upon the face between the half-timber construction of the structure. About 1720 John Turner (the son) improved his dwelling by replacing the original casements with double hung windows, and covering the old frame and walls with plaster and the very fine panelwork that the dwelling now displays.

With the Narbonne House, built before 1671, on Essex Street, nearby, the John Ward House, and the Seven Gables group, the visitor to Salem may obtain an excellent idea of the type of seventeenth-century architecture that prevailed in New England during the years of its settlement. This understanding may be further strengthened by a visit to the Pioneer Village in nearby Forest River Park — where some early Puritan houses and colonial industries were set up for the Salem Tercentenary celebration.

Following these seventeenth-century houses, Salem also presents a group representative of the early part of the succeeding century. Of these the Ropes Memorial, built about 1719, is most easily available to visi-

House — for the temporary common housing of all the group employed upon the venture.

Turning now to the John Turner House next door, we may deal with more definite and tangible facts. John Turner built his house — the first portion of it — in 1668. At that time he purchased the land, with a "single house" upon it (a house with one room upon each floor, and two and a half stories high, with a large chimney — and stairs in front of it — at one end), which he took down and rebuilt — possibly using part of the old frame — with the hall, or living room, upon the west side of the chimney and the kitchen upon the east. The house then had four gables; two upon the front and one at each end (as in the John Ward House, 1684, back of the Essex Institute). The original hall is the present dining room. Shortly after, in 1678, the large south wing, with parlor and bedroom over it was built, with higher ceilings and roof than in the original building. At this time, too, the entrance must have been extended to the south on both floors.

Up to this time the interior of the house had probably been walled with wide pine boards, with "shadow

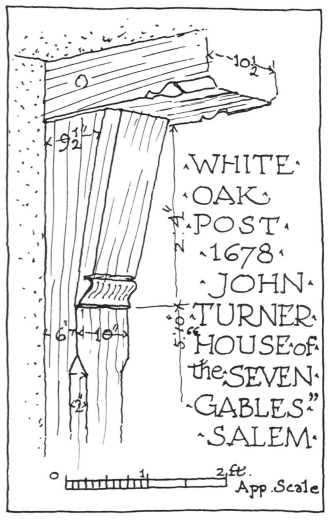

·WHITE· ·OAK· ·POST· ·1678· ·JOHN· ·TURNER· ·HOUSE·of· the·SEVEN· ·GABLES·" ·SALEM·

App. Scale

Southeasterly Portion Thought to be Gov. Endecott's Dwelling Erected in 1624
HOOPER-HATHAWAY HOUSE — 1682 — SALEM, MASSACHUSETTS

JOHN TURNER HOUSE (HOUSE OF THE SEVEN GABLES)—1668—TURNER STREET, SALEM, MASSACHUSETTS

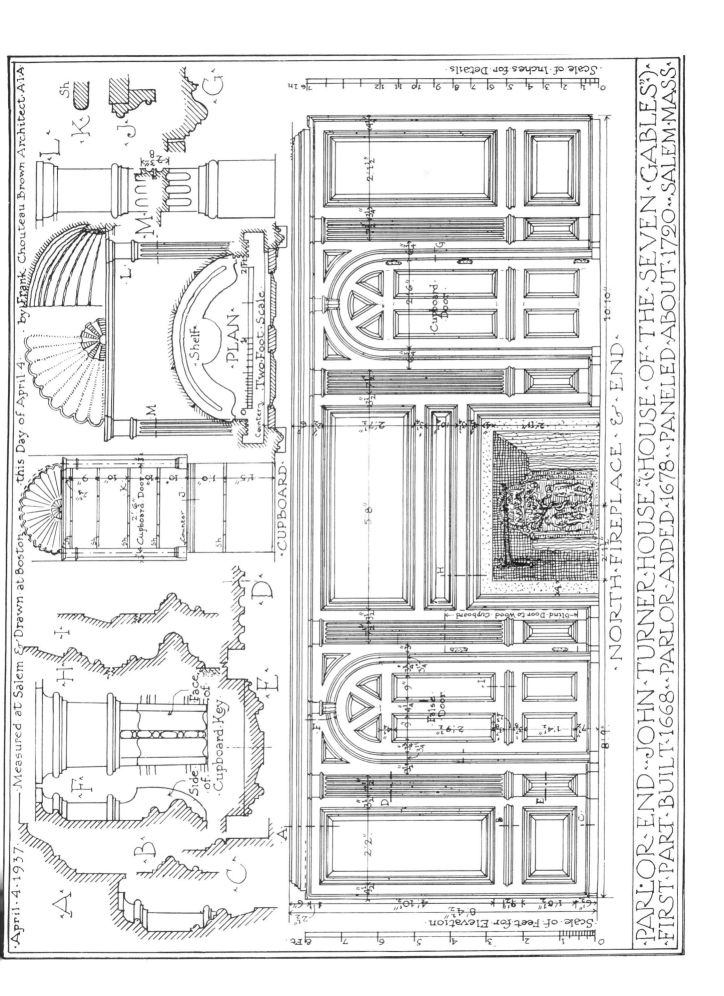

·PARLOR·OR·END··JOHN·TURNER·HOUSE··"HOUSE·OF·THE·SEVEN·GABLES"··
·FIRST·PART·BUILT·1668··PARLOR·ADDED·1678··PANELED·ABOUT·1720···SALEM·MASS·

tors, and contains exceptional fittings and furnishings, with a nice old garden behind a fine fence, at the side.

The earliest brick house in Salem is the Derby House, built in 1762 by Capt. Richard Derby, near the head of Derby Wharf. Its beautiful paneled interiors, and the old wooden Counting House beside the doorway, may be incorporated into the Permanent Memorial, with famous Derby Wharf restored, and the Federal Custom House of 1819 (see Volume X,

by the execrable masonry of its recent WPA "restoration"); the Hamilton Hall (Volume X, Chapter 8), the beautiful South Church that formerly stood across the street, built in 1804–1805, by McIntire, which burned December 19, 1903; the Pierce-Johonnot-Nichols House, 1782, with its sturdy McIntire façade and picturesque stables and court yard; the Pingree House, 1810, by McIntire, next door to the Essex Institute, with its beautifully furnished rooms; the Cook-Oliver House,

Parlor End

JOHN TURNER HOUSE (HOUSE OF THE SEVEN GABLES), SALEM, MASSACHUSETTS

Chapter 8) nearby. Besides this, an earlier but little known Custom House, built in 1805, also exists off Essex Street.

But after all, Salem is better known for its architecture of the later and more elaborate period, when Samuel McIntire and his associate carvers were in their prime. During the years that brought about the turn of the century into the eighteenth, Mr. Samuel McIntire was as much in demand in Salem as was Bulfinch in Boston. To this period belongs the fine brick Town House, 1817 (now unfortunately marred

whose interior is supposed to contain much of the McIntire finish taken from Elias Haskett Derby's elaborate Town House, built 1799, when it was demolished in 1815.

While Chestnut Street contains some of the best houses of the late Salem period, in summer they are mostly obscured by the thick foliage of beautiful trees, that do much to add charm and appeal to that stately avenue—and the houses bounding on Washington Square, in another—and less regarded—part of the town, are also among the most imposing in the city.

WASHINGTON SQUARE NORTH, SALEM, MASSACHUSETTS

CHESTNUT STREET, SALEM, MASSACHUSETTS

Entrance Detail
CAPT. JOSEPH WATERS HOUSE — 1806–1807 — 29 WASHINGTON SQUARE NORTH,
SALEM, MASSACHUSETTS

COOK-OLIVER HOUSE—1782—FEDERAL STREET, SALEM, MASSACHUSETTS
Samuel McIntire, Architect

ROPES MEMORIAL—ABOUT 1719—ESSEX STREET, SALEM, MASSACHUSETTS

Old Counting House at the Left of Picture

CAPT. RICHARD DERBY HOUSE—1762—NEAR THE HEAD OF DERBY WHARF, SALEM, MASSACHUSETTS

Porch
HOUSE AT 380 ESSEX STREET, SALEM, MASSACHUSETTS
Samuel McIntire, Architect

Stables and Court Yard
PIERCE-JOHONNOT-NICHOLS HOUSE, SALEM, MASSACHUSETTS
Samuel McIntire, Architect

PIERCE-JOHONNOT-NICHOLS HOUSE — 1782 — FEDERAL STREET, SALEM, MASSACHUSETTS
Samuel McIntire, Architect

Danvers, Massachusetts
Part One

Text by
Frank Chouteau Brown
Photographs by
Arthur C. Haskell
Originally published in 1938 as White Pine Monograph
Volume XXIV, Number 5

ELIAS ENDICOTT PORTER FARMHOUSE—1737—LOCUST STREET, PUTNAMVILLE,
DANVERS, MASSACHUSETTS

DANVERS (OLD SALEM VILLAGE), MASSACHUSETTS, PART ONE

STEMMING, as the township of Danvers does, so directly from the Salem settlement, it follows that much of its early beginnings already has been disclosed in the previous chapter. It was one of the many townships that were later set apart from the area originally established, as within the Naumkeag (later to be known as the Salem) settlement. As they exist today, Danvers includes a portion of the land that was the original "Salem Village," or "Farms"; which also then included most of the present area of Peabody, which lies between Danvers and Salem to the south and east.

Beverly and Wenham also extend along its eastern side, with Wenham and Topsfield on the north; and Topsfield and Middleton on the west. All these townships also were included in the original Salem, with the addition of Manchester and Marblehead, although it only included a part of Topsfield. Indeed, the original grant, given by "the Council for New England" to Endecott and the Dorchester Company included most of Essex County—and parts of Norfolk, Suffolk and Middlesex, as well!

Later, in 1629, the Charter of King Charles the First, gave to "the Governor and Company of the Massachusetts Bay in New England" power for its "freemen" to elect annually their own Governor, Deputy, and eighteen Assistants—who made up "the Great and General Court," with authority to establish laws over the new settlement. It was true that a "freeman" had to be also a member of the established church, in good and regular standing, but, when it was discovered that these elections had been taken over by the settlers themselves (whereas it had evidently been originally intended that the electoral government would be handled altogether by the English members of the Company); it was arranged—after fifty-five years of operation—to substitute another charter, with rather less liberal terms, for the earlier document of the Council for New England.

Peabody remained a part of the Danvers area until 1855, when it became a separate township. It had

formerly been known as Brooksby. And Danvers did not secure its full and complete independence as a township, even in 1752, when, after a long struggle for separation from Salem, it was granted separate town government. But only as a district without individual representation in the General Court.

Although the first profitable industry of the Salem settlement was fishing, it was not long before a large part of this business was taken over by the Marblehead community and about Salem Harbor there gradually developed the more profitable business of maritime merchandising on the larger scale available at the time, until the town's piers and warehouses were soon handling the products of the ports of all the world. But, meanwhile, there was also the need of growing the farm produce necessary to maintain the daily life of the settlement, and it was soon discovered that the region about the harbor was none too fertile, and the land none too well adapted to this purpose. And so Salem Village—or the Farms—became the farming center of the settlement. There, on land adjacent to the harbor, to the north and west, was much rich soil disposed upon gently rolling hillsides and fertile valleys, and more protected from the sometimes boisterous winds and storms along the seacoast.

Gov. John Endecott had in 1632 been granted by the General Court, a large farmstead for himself in what is now Danversport, in recognition of his services to the colony. He called it Little Orchard Farm and a part of the original property was still owned by the late William C. Endicott, at the time of his death a year or two ago. Governor Endecott ordered fruit trees from England and by 1640 had planted a large orchard, of which the famous Endecott Pear Tree may be now the sole survivor.

In fact, three early grants comprised most of the present areas of Danversport and Peabody. Besides the Endecott lands, these included the grant to the Rev. Samuel Skelton, (made in July, 1632) and that to John Humphrey (1635) which extended nearly to the Lynnfield boundary. From 1635 on, many additional interior land grants were made to those families who wished to carry on farming in the community. Thus, by 1638 there was a well-defined separate settlement in the Village or Farms area, first established under the Rev. John Phillips, who later returned to England. These later grants of farm lands were all made by the Salem selectmen, including one (made about 1640) to John Putnam—whose family name has since become indissolubly associated with the history of the town, as well as that of the Commonwealth and the country during the Revolution.

About 1644 another grant of some 300 acres was made to John Porter, in Danvers Plains, and he was later credited with establishing the first tannery.

After several petitions to the Salem fathers, in 1672 the Salem Village Parish was allowed to be organized. This included Danvers—outside the Port—about half of Peabody, and a part of Beverly. The word "parish," as used in this connection meant rather a "town" than a "church," so that from that time on until 1752, when Danvers was finally "set off" from Salem, the parish records actually were the records of the town.

In 1673 was built the first Meeting House, a structure of 34 x 28 feet,

GEORGE JACOBS HOUSE
DANVERSPORT, MASSACHUSETTS

on a site that has been identified as in a field now near the corner of Hobart and Forest streets. The old Training Field for the militia company organized in 1671, was the Common at Danvers Highlands, given to the town in 1709 by Deacon Nathaniel Ingersoll. A few years later, in 1676, a Watch House was erected on Watch House Hill, an eminence about at the Highlands parsonage pasture, although the church in this section was not organized until 1689.

In the "Witchcraft Delusion," which flourished in Salem Village in 1692, the First Village Meeting House—which was also used as the Town House

of the community was employed for the "examination" of some of the victims—and it may have been partly to help forget this regrettable hysteria that a new Meeting House was begun in 1700, on Watch House Hill. It was a structure that has been described as nearly square in plan (the dimensions having been 48 x 43 feet) and built at a cost of £330. It had a hip roof of the rather steep pitch of the period, a tower or cupola story rising from the center of the roof, and interior galleries. It continued in use until 1752 and was finally demolished in 1786. In 1710, the Middle Precinct was given permission to build its own church; and by 1711 a new Meeting House, 51 by 38 feet, had been constructed. The contributing area included what is now known as Peabody and a part of Middleton (which was not set apart until 1728), then known as Mills Hill. Finally, in 1752, the District of Danvers was incorporated, but without being given the privilege of a delegate to the General Court. The town records show that at that time there were 25 slaves living within the new District limits.

In connection with the "Witchcraft Delusion," there remain three structures in which dwelt individuals whose names were associated with its history. The Sarah Prince-Osborn House, 1660, now at 273 Maple Street, but formerly on Spring Street, has been both moved and remodeled. Sarah Osborn was among the first accused, was tried on March 1, and died while in Boston Jail the following May. Rebecca Nurse was the fourth woman accused by Tituba, a West Indian slave of the Rev. Samuel Parris, minister of the Salem Village church, in whose household the delusion originated. Rebecca Nurse was then seventy years old, and lived in an old house off Pine Street, built in 1678, which was rather too thoroughly "restored" in 1909; but which nevertheless still provides a good popular idea of the appearance of a seventeenth-century dwelling. She was hanged July 19, 1692, and her body placed

View of North Side Showing Lean-to at Rear

View of Rear and West End
REBECCA NURSE HOUSE — 1678 — DANVERS, MASSACHUSETTS

in the family burying ground, now to be found in a field near some pines off Collins Street.

The third, the George Jacobs House, is now in process of disintegration, having been abandoned several years ago after a fire that damaged one end. Jacobs was tried and hanged on August 19, 1692. The remains of the Jacobs House, built about 1658, may still be seen in a field overlooking Waters' River, looking out toward the Beverly shore to the east, and the

Another principal association of this area is concerned with its occupancy by Gen. Thomas Gage, the last Provincial Governor of Massachusetts, during 1774, just previous to the Revolution. He resided at "The Lindens," a fine house built for a summer residence by Robert ("King") Hooper of Marblehead, in 1754, and a room in the Col. Jeremiah Page House, a narrow gambrel dwelling built about 1754 and formerly facing on Danvers Square, (but now removed

GENERAL ISRAEL PUTNAM HOUSE — DANVERS, MASSACHUSETTS
Older Part at Rear — 1648. Front Portion Added 1744

original Little Orchard Farm of Governor Endecott, with the three-story Reed-Porter House (Volume IX, Chapter 7) there named the Crowninshield House, after Benjamin Crowninshield, one of its occupants) in the foreground to the west. Even in its final stages it displays the sturdy construction of its time, with the heavy pinned framework, brick nogged, still resisting the untimely results of its exposure to the weather through all the years.

to 11 Page Street for the headquarters of the Danvers Historical Society), for his office, because of its view over Salem Harbor.

But probably the name most generally and widely associated with the town of Danvers is that of the Putnam family of Revolutionary fame, of whose houses there still remain a large number in this township. The two doorways measured for this chapter, (from the Col. Jesse Putnam and Samuel Putnam

South Front

Rear With Lean-to and Vestibules
COL. JESSE PUTNAM HOUSE — c1750 — DANVERS, MASSACHUSETTS

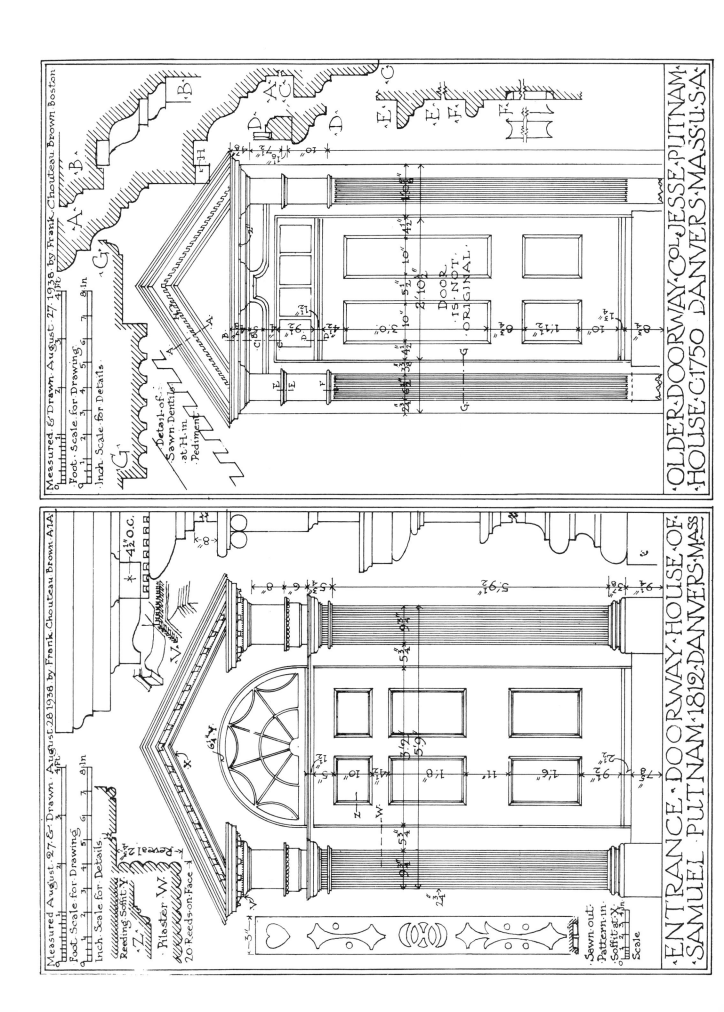

Measured & Drawn August 27. 1938. by Frank Chouteau Brown Boston

Foot Scale for Drawing

Inch Scale for Details

Detail of Sawn Dentils at H. in Pediment

DOOR IS NOT ORIGINAL

OLDER DOORWAY CO: JESSE PUTNAM HOUSE C1750 DANVERS MASS USA

Measured August 27 & Drawn August 28 1938 by Frank Chouteau Brown A1A

Foot Scale for Drawing

Inch Scale for Details

Reeding Soffit Y
Pilaster W
20 Reeds on Face
Reveal 2

Sawn out Pattern in Soffit at X
Scale

ENTRANCE DOORWAY HOUSE OF SAMUEL PUTNAM 1812 DANVERS MASS

Older Doorway

JESSE PUTNAM HOUSE—c1750—DANVERS, MASSACHUSETTS

Entrance Doorway

SAMUEL PUTNAM HOUSE—1812—DANVERS, MASSACHUSETTS

houses) show an early and a late example, of which the latter displays a few typical details and mouldings found repeated in many other houses in the vicinity.

Danvers also provides several examples of "double" houses, one being the Col. Jesse Putnam Farmhouse (1750), a short distance beyond which is the Joseph Putnam House, where Gen. Israel Putnam was born, near the old Newburyport turnpike. The older part (1648) of this latter house is at the rear, there having

two more rooms, added across the rear of the older portion; the whole still being enclosed by a wide gambrel rather than merely a lean-to, in order to secure two full-height rooms across the rear upon the second floor.

The Elias E. Porter Farmhouse on Locust Street, although having a flat sloping roof with end gables, also grew to its present size in exactly the same way; by the same first three steps of enlargement. To that outline, however, some owner also added a semi-

Southeast Room on First Floor
JAMES PUTNAM HOUSE, DANVERS, MASSACHUSETTS

been a newer portion (added in 1744) built entirely across the front toward the street.

The James Putnam House (which is located about midway between the two other houses of the same family just mentioned, but a little way from the main highway), gained its present sizeable gambrel by degrees. It was probably first a two-story "one-room" house; then widened by the addition of another room, adding to the width of its front. Later, the old narrow gambrel was heightened and widened to cover

lean-to extending partly across the rear of the house, and a finely proportioned end vestibule. The northern end of this house has the unusual fenestration of five narrow fifteen-light windows on both the first and second floors, and this farm at one time boasted twenty-seven buildings! Much of the interior detail dates from its later enlargement (probably about 1810 to 1815) and is of unusual delicacy, while it also displays many of the characteristic local details so evidently favored by Danvers' builders.

South Front

East Gable End
JAMES PUTNAM HOUSE, DANVERS, MASSACHUSETTS

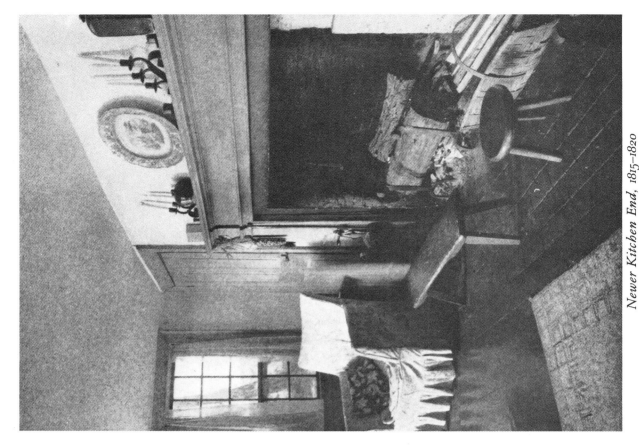

Newer Kitchen End, 1815–1820

Dining Room

ELIAS ENDICOTT PORTER FARMHOUSE—1737—LOCUST STREET, DANVERS, MASSACHUSETTS

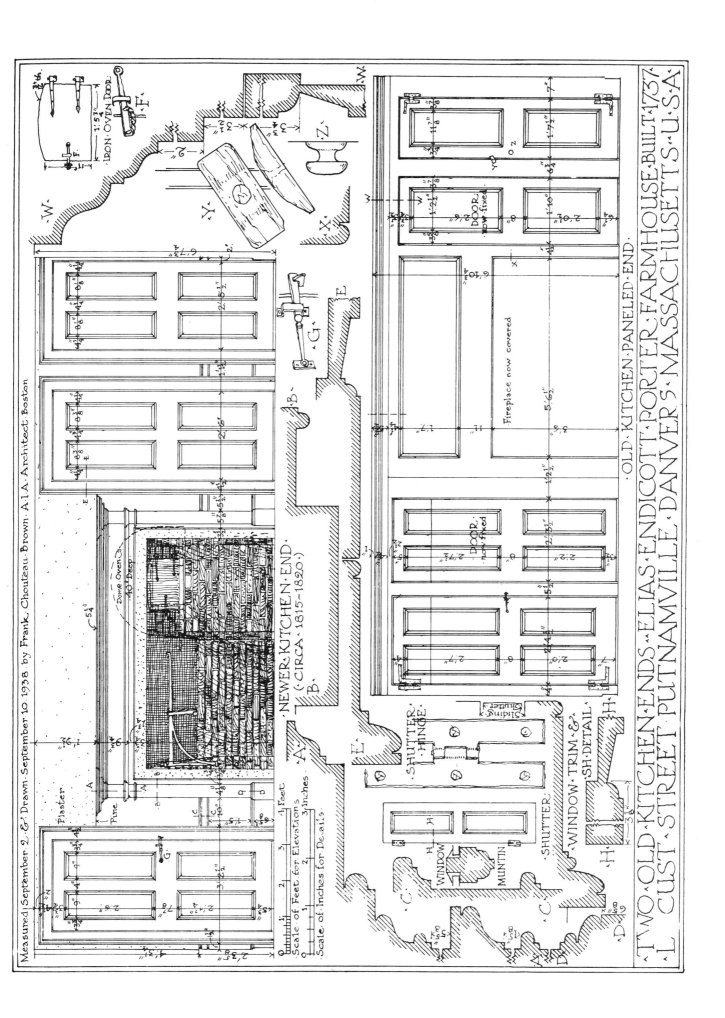

- TWO - OLD - KITCHEN - ENDS - ELIAS - ENDICOTT - PORTER - FARMHOUSE - BUILT 1737 -
- L - CUST - STREET - PUTNAMVILLE - DANVERS - MASSACHUSETTS - U.S.A.

House and Barns

Farm Buildings

ELIAS ENDICOTT PORTER FARM — 1737 — LOCUST STREET, PUTNAMVILLE,
DANVERS, MASSACHUSETTS

Entrance Hall
"THE LINDENS"—1754—FORMERLY AT DANVERS, MASSACHUSETTS

Detail of Front
"THE LINDENS"—1754—FORMERLY AT DANVERS, MASSACHUSETTS

Danvers, Massachusetts
Part Two

Text by
Frank Chouteau Brown
Photographs by
Arthur C. Haskell
Originally published in 1938 as White Pine Monograph
Volume XXIV, Number 6

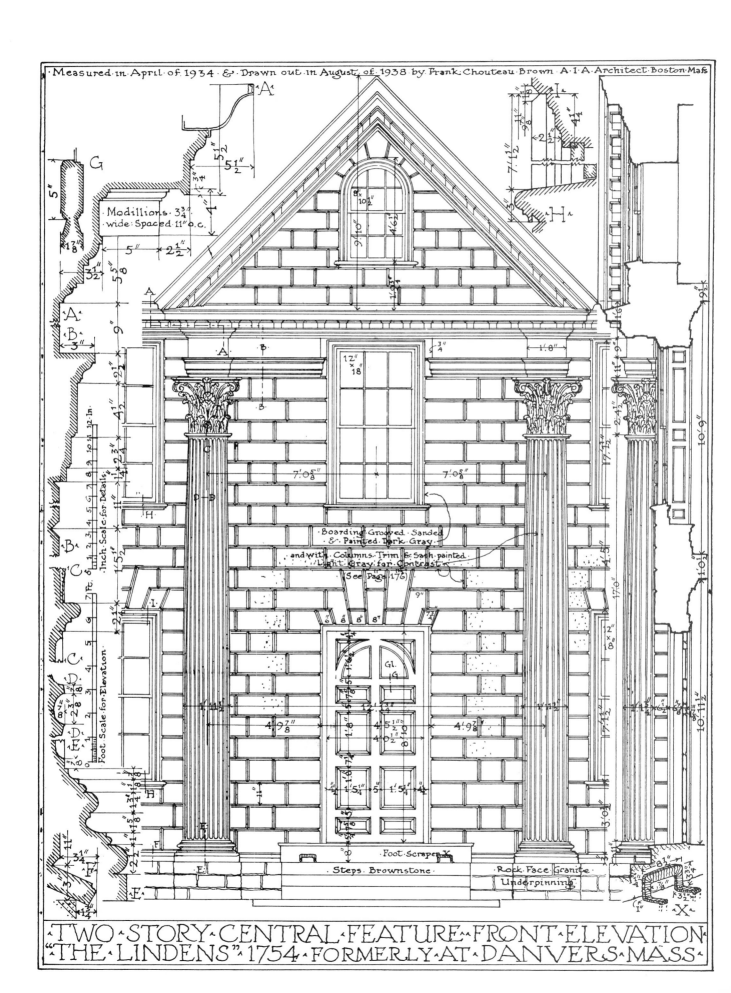

Measured in April of 1934 & Drawn out in August of 1938 by Frank Chouteau Brown A.I.A. Architect Boston Mass.

Modillions 3¾ wide Spaced 11" o.c.

Boarding Grooved Sanded & Painted Dark Gray and with Columns Trim & Sash painted Light Gray for Contrast. (See Page 176)

Foot Scraper X

Steps Brownstone.

Rock Face Granite Underpinning

·TWO·STORY·CENTRAL·FEATURE·FRONT·ELEVATION·
"THE·LINDENS"·1754·FORMERLY·AT·DANVERS·MASS·

DANVERS (OLD SALEM VILLAGE), MASSACHUSETTS, PART TWO

OVER most of the area of early Salem (Naumkeag) not much original structural work remains. Business has of recent years pretty well supplanted many old buildings over large sections of what is now the more populous part of Salem, Beverly, and Peabody. Then, twenty-four years ago, there was the Salem fire, that swept away a large residential area of that center and the waterfront almost up to the Custom House and Derby Wharf locations—the latter now in process of rebuilding by the Federal Government. We must turn, therefore, to the former less-built-up region of the Farms, to find the greatest number of local examples of dwellings built previous to the nineteenth century, as well as those that are perhaps less well-known and less familiar to the casual visitor, or even, to the usual student.

So, leaving Salem—as well as the seaside margins of Marblehead and Beverly—and turning inland toward the west, and north, and skirting the shores and inlets of Beverly Bay upon the right, one today still follows the ancient highway from Salem to Danvers and Danversport.

After passing the Jacob's house location in the fields on the right, and the three-story Reed-Crownin-shield-Porter dwelling at Danversport upon the left, just before the roadway makes a sharp right-angle turn, near the head of the inlet from Beverly Harbor, are the "twin houses," side by side, overlooking Crane River inlet and the old shipyard sites, built by Captains John and Moses Endicott, probably dating from about 1798. The vestibules of these houses have already been recorded both in photographs and measured drawings, in "A Group of Eastern Massachusetts Vestibules" (Volume I, Chapter 8).

Beyond the center—and rather different from any other example of dwellings within the old Salem area—is the house built about 1784 by the Rev. Benjamin Wadsworth, near the old parsonage site, now Centre Street. While not exactly a common type in New England, it is nevertheless, in its sturdy and vigorous detail, and in the somewhat unusual combination of hip-and-gambrel roof lines, a form of dwelling that indubitably belongs to the period of the Revolution,

or within the short decade following.

After passing The Mills and Danvers Square, both north and west the agricultural character of this region has been well maintained over all the years between its original settlement and the present date. The oldest structures are to be found along some of the older roads, or down rutted lanes and driveways, where old groves of trees and clustering overgrown shrubs suggest the location of early dwellings to one experienced in such a quest. Even then one meets many disappointments; for far too many of the old sites have been usurped by later buildings, or the old house—if it is still to be traced at all—has been surrounded by newer ells and additions, and often entirely rebuilt to suit the requirements of more recent owners. Such a Danvers house was Oak Hill, for instance, set far back from the road, in mid-Victorian ugliness, but yet containing the remnants of an older dwelling; including two rooms by Samuel McIntire, that now fortunately have been transplanted to a more accessible and safer location in the Boston Art Museum. As the building had been sold to be adapted to other purposes, this removal, at least, was justified.

Less happy was the fate of "The Lindens." Built as the country place of the Hon. Robert (better known as "King") Hooper of Marblehead in 1754, it was—in its chosen setting of gardens, and linden-planted approach—a noble example of a fine New England dwelling of the period. Its dignified design and finish, high ceilings, and rooms with four-paneled walls, marked it as one of the best in all that countryside. But it fell upon evil days. It was purchased as a gamble by second-hand furniture dealers. It was up for sale, piecemeal or wholesale, over several years. One fine interior went to a Middle Western museum. The room paneling was cheaply reproduced and (so rumor hath it) sold again! And, finally, a purchaser for what remained was found; and now the site shows only the remains of the trees and the old garden—and a gaping cellar hole! The dwelling has been re-erected upon a closely crowded urban lot in a semi-Southern city—far from "its own, its native land" with much of its glamour and glory reft ruthlessly away!

"The Lindens" formerly on Sylvan Street, on land that was part of the original Endecott grant and sometimes known as the Governor's Plains, had a stairway that was second in beauty and spaciousness only to that in the hallway of the Lee Mansion in Marblehead; and the first and second hall wall covering was also reminiscent of the treatment that may still be seen in the Marblehead mansion. But in its exterior design, the gambreled Danvers dwelling pos-

Haskett Derby of Salem, and developed as his summer estate by Samuel McIntire. It was here that the charming, unusual two-story summerhouse was built at the cost of £100 and completed by McIntire in July, 1793. In 1901, it was moved four miles across country, and has since that time decorated the Endicott gardens at Danvers. This structure is illustrated in Volume IX, Chapter 8, and combines the favorite archway feature—employed so frequently by McIntire to focus the vista beyond a garden approach—

"THE LINDENS", FORMERLY AT DANVERS, NOW IN WASHINGTON, D.C.

sessed an unusual facade; having a central feature, with two engaged Corinthian columns and steep-pitched pediment (a truly unique treatment, shown in detail in the measured drawing on page 56 and the views on pages 54 and 58 along with four richly-moulded dormers and a decorative roof balustrade.

The house was purchased from the Hooper heirs in 1797—a few years after its builder's death—by Judge Benajah Collins, related to the local Eppes family; whose farm, now in Peabody, was purchased by Elias

upon the lower story, with diminutive rooms on either side, from one of which rises the stairway to the upper floor, which provided a summer garden room to overlook gardens and pleasance on all four sides. The pilastered second story is surmounted by a pedimented roof treatment, with two Watteau-like carved figures, and corner pedestals with finely turned vases—the whole most exquisitely and delicately proportioned and scaled.

There were also three McIntire mantels that—at

JUDGE SAMUEL HOLTEN HOUSE, DANVERS, MASSACHUSETTS

some injury to the original paneling — were somewhat arbitrarily incorporated by Francis Peabody into "The Lindens," when he owned the place in 1860; two from his grandfather's house in Salem, and one from Oak Hill, added in 1873. The two McIntire mantels from the Joseph Peabody House were placed in the room at the right of the entrance on the first floor, and in the bedroom on the right at the head of the stairs. The mantel from Oak Hill was located in the northwest bedroom on the second floor. It was during his occupancy that the gardens also were ex-

to have been located upon the site. Often that portion first built was but as large upon the ground as a single room, facing toward the south, with a large fireplace and constricted staircase upon one or the other end. The structure was often two stories and attic high; sometimes only a story and a half cottage. In either case, the easiest and most obvious first enlargement of its size was to add to its length, thus making full use of the original stairs and chimney, for both old and new rooms, upon both floor levels.

As in the case of this dwelling the various additions

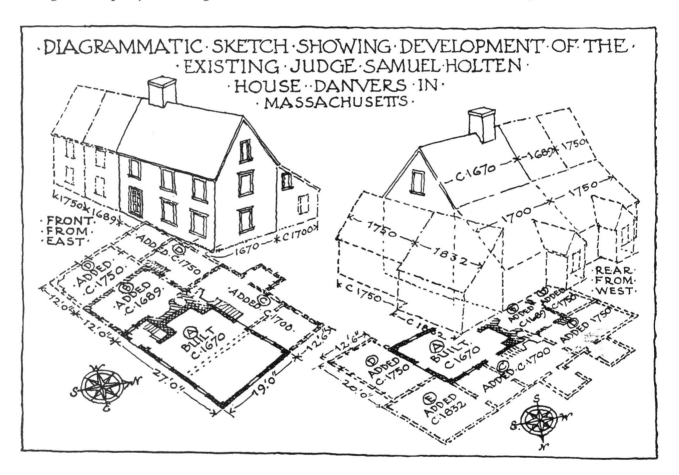

tended somewhat to the west, over the site of the original slave quarters.

In the preceding chapter were noted two examples of Danvers dwellings that had grown from one-room houses to full farmstead size — as well as the local prevalence of double-house plans. In this chapter is shown one of the best known and most interesting cases of a similar growth; the Judge Samuel Holten House. Many an old dwelling is known, or suspected, to have evolved in much the same way!

It is, of course, customary, when quoting a date for an old building, to give that of the oldest part known

have been fairly definitely determined, and although there still remains some doubt as to the exact years in which each addition was made, it illustrates this "progressive development" which can be suspected — and sometimes traced — in many other old New England dwellings. The portion first built, probably erected by Benjamin Holten (also sometimes spelled "Houlton") about 1670, was a typical one-room-house plan, with one room on each of two floors, and an attic, and a large chimney and stairs at the southwest end. The first addition was made about 1689, and consisted of another room adding to the

View from South

View from West
JUDGE SAMUEL HOLTEN HOUSE, DANVERS, MASSACHUSETTS

structure's length, upon the other side of the chimney and stairs. But instead of being as large or even, as was most usual, a little larger than the earlier room — the new room was smaller and of less width upon the front. This extended the roof ridge and the front of the house about twelve feet more to the southwest.

The next addition (the second) was also made in the usual way, in about 1700. It was the regular lean-to at the rear. Again it was not *quite* the usual thing — as it only extended as far as the original one-

the end gable house wall, extending beyond the front wall of the dwelling, to shelter an outside door and make a short "Beverly jog." This room was probably intended to provide Judge Holten with an office; and it may have been a few years apart from the extension to the southwest, in which case it might have been the fourth addition made to the original plan!

Again, in 1832 — or thereabouts — another room was added in the indented north corner of the house; and probably the front vestibule was made, by moving

Entrance Hall and Stair
JUDGE SAMUEL HOLTEN HOUSE, DANVERS, MASSACHUSETTS

room portion, and the roof was established at a slightly flatter slope than that upon the main house. The third addition was made about fifteen years later, when the building was largely rebuilt, perhaps in 1752. It consisted of another room on the southwest end, (again adding about twelve feet to the length of the house front and to its ridge) and the extension of the rear lean-to at the same time, while another lean-to was built against the northeast end, but to quite different effect, as here the roof sloped up against

out the old front door and adding another beside it, at about the same time. These last changes were made after the death of its most famous occupant, Judge Samuel Holten, in January, 1816, when he was 78 years old.

He had been a member of the State Provincial Congresses of 1768 and 1775; a member of the General Committee of Safety; representative of Massachusetts at the Yorktown Convention of 1777, when he helped in framing the Articles of Federation; President of

Double Privy at Rear of Dwelling
JUDGE SAMUEL HOLTEN HOUSE, DANVERS, MASSACHUSETTS

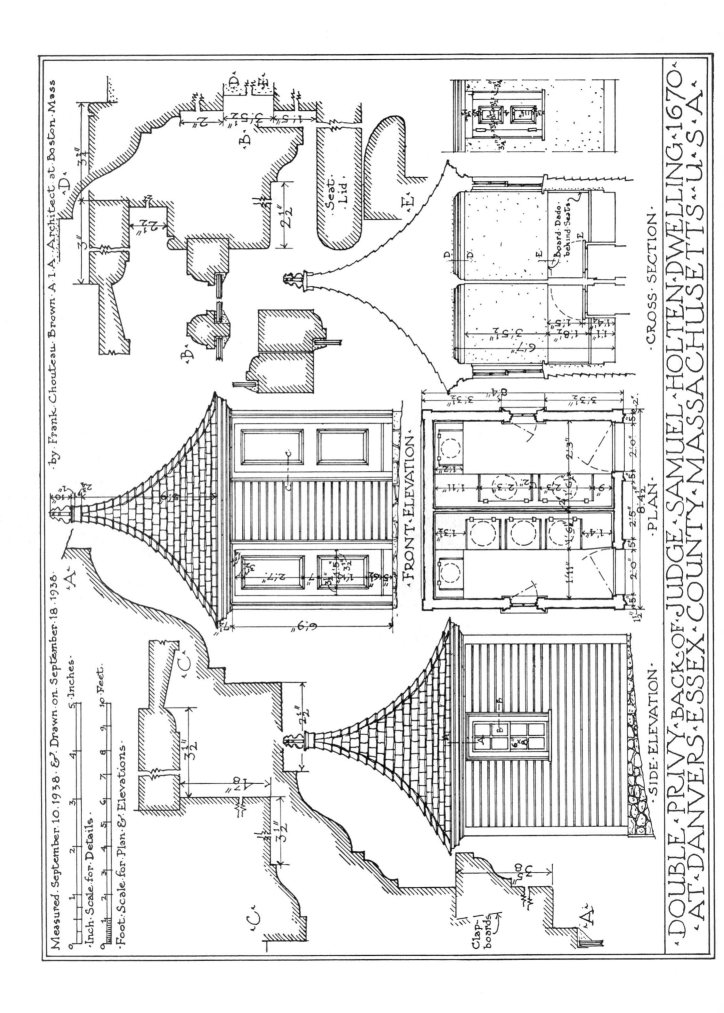

·D·

·B·

Seat.
Lid.

·E·

·B·

·A·

Board Dado
behind Seats

E

D

D

E

·CROSS·SECTION·

· by·Frank·Chouteau·Brown·A·1·A··Architect·at·Boston·Mass

·Measured·September·10·1938·&·Drawn·on·September·18·1938·

·A·

·Inch·Scale·for·Details·

·Foot·Scale·for·Plan·&·Elevations·

c

·FRONT·ELEVATION·

·PLAN·

·C·

·C·

·SIDE·ELEVATION·

A

B

6"×8"

Clap-
boards

·A·

·DOUBLE·PRIVY·BACK·OF·JUDGE·SAMUEL·HOLTEN·DWELLING·1670·
·AT·DANVERS·ESSEX·COUNTY·MASSACHUSETTS·U·S·A·

SAMUEL FOWLER HOUSE—1809—HIGH AND LIBERTY STREETS, DANVERS, MASSACHUSETTS

View of Stair Hall

4'-7" x 6'-10" x ⅞" Door

SAMUEL FOWLER HOUSE—1809—HIGH AND LIBERTY STREETS, DANVERS, MASSACHUSETTS

Southwest Room, First Floor

View across Entrance Hallway

SAMUEL FOWLER HOUSE—1809—HIGH AND LIBERTY STREETS, DANVERS, MASSACHUSETTS

the Continental Congress in 1785; thirty-two years Judge of Essex County Court of Common Pleas; thirty-five years Judge of General Sessions, for fifteen of which he was acting Chief Justice; also occupant of many honored positions in the town—selectman, moderator, treasurer, etc., and served five years in the State Senate and twelve years on the Governor's Council.

He left his house to his daughter, Mary Putnam, and his granddaughter, Mary Ann Putnam; and it is

and Liberty streets, is a fine example of New England restraint in material and design. Built at a period when, especially in this locality, local builders and ship-craftsmen had developed a large number of delicately-worked variants of ornamental wood mouldings, its selection of material had largely eliminated this type of ornament and fallen back instead upon sheer, chaste beauty of proportion and composition. So this dwelling can be accepted as perhaps typical of

Side View across Yard
SAMUEL FOWLER HOUSE—1809—DANVERS, MASSACHUSETTS

probable that the double vestibule and privy date from about that time, or perhaps a little later, in 1823.

Samuel Fowler, born 1776 and died 1859, built the simple square brick house known by his name, in 1809. His father had owned and conducted a shipyard at the New Mills; and he continued as mill owner, as well as operating a large tannery near Liberty Bridge. This dwelling, on the corner of High

the severely simple type of brick dwelling architecture of that period, of which elsewhere within its limits the same township furnishes several other, although smaller, instances of structures employing the same material and a nearly similar simplicity of design.

It is now among the several structures owned by the Society for the Preservation of New England Antiquities, representing different cultural periods, and is one of the most consistently perfect of them all.

Both in its architecture and furnishing it is of a simplicity that seems quite *un*architectural in all its means. Not the least of its appeal to the appreciative student is the number of original wall papers that have been preserved upon its rooms, including one scenic paper decorating the parlor.

This paper is believed to have been among the first printed by Jean Zuber et Cie, who while still using many small wood blocks for the many colors of their

which was immediately accepted and has continued in use until today.

The painted designs of the wall decorations in the hall and principal rooms of the Lee Mansion, in Marblehead, were made upon sheets of paper about 26″ x 22″. This work in style recalls French *grisaille* painting, while the Classic forms employed in the design also suggest French decorators or, possibly, English copyists as their origin. The other wall coverings

Near the Old Parsonage Site, Now Centre Street
WADSWORTH HOUSE — c1784 — DANVERS, MASSACHUSETTS

patterns, were the first to combine these printings upon continuous rolls of paper to be applied perpendicularly. Previously all wall paper printings had been made upon squares of paper usually about 15″ x 19″ to 18″ x 22″. Then these were separately pasted upon the wall to make up the panel of the design. The change was made by Zuber about 1829 and its obvious convenience and saving of time in application made it an advance in the manufacture of wall paper,

in the Fowler House are of more conventional pattern and simpler coloring, of which the coldly Classical or Adam-like character of that on the hall is perhaps unusually successful in striking the identical note in decoration that is to be discerned in the architectural restraint of the exterior, in the precise, yet attenuated mouldings of the staircase, mantels and, indeed, of all the woodwork of the interior, as may be seen in the photographic views reproduced herewith.

COTTAGE, HOBART STREET, DANVERS, MASSACHUSETTS

COTTAGE, SYLVAN STREET, DANVERS, MASSACHUSETTS

Watertown, Massachusetts

Text by
Frank Chouteau Brown
Photographs by
Arthur C. Haskell
Originally published in 1937 as White Pine Monograph
Volume XXIII, Number 3

GOLDEN BALL TAVERN—1753—CENTRAL AVENUE, WESTON, MASSACHUSETTS

WATERTOWN, MASSACHUSETTS

W HEN Governor Winthrop arrived in Salem, Massachusetts, on June 12, 1630, Sir Richard Saltonstall was among his following. Not caring for the conditions they found existing in that colony, shortly after their arrival, on June 17, Governor Winthrop and Sir Richard started out to find some better location in which they could settle—and Winthrop tells in his journal that "We went to Mattachusetts" (as Boston Harbor was known at that time) "to find out a place for our settleing down. We went up Mistick River about six miles. We lay at Mr. Mavericks and returned home Saturday." On July 1 he tells us that the *Mayflower* and *Whale* had arrived safe in Charlestown Harbor— being followed by the *Talbot* on the 2nd, and the *Trial* upon the 5th—where John Endecott (to forestall an anticipated similar enterprise by Gorges men from the northern settlements) had previously made a small settlement and started the building of the Great House at Mishawan (Charlestown), to which the new settlers decided to come. And accordingly, at Charlestown were landed most of the passengers arriving on the four vessels named and the balance of the 1630 fleet.

As has been told elsewhere, they shortly thereafter removed from Charlestown to Boston, but meanwhile many of the large company—by some counts numbering nearly fifteen hundred souls—had gradually scattered and found themselves locations in the country roundabout. Sir Richard Saltonstall, either at the time of his expedition of June 17, with Gov. Winthrop, or later, explored further up the Charles River, and was so impressed by the rich meadows found on tidal water, only five to six miles above the harbor, that within forty-eight days after the arrival of the *Arbella* at Salem, or by August 1, 1630, he was organizing—along with thirty-nine others—a church at Watertown, which was the third to be set up in Puritan New England.

If Salem is to be regarded as the first settlement made (after Plymouth), upon Massachusetts Bay, and the Charlestown-Boston one the next in order—then Watertown would become the third. It is true that Dorchester was settled in between, but the first group did not remain as a permanent settlement, and the place was resettled later with new arrivals, largely from Boston itself, with which Dorchester afterwards was joined. The large part of the original Dorchester group departed in 1636 to resettle in Windsor, Connecticut—including almost the entire congregation of Rev. Philip Hooker; who was at the head of the second Church established in the colony, the first having been set up at Salem.

No exact date for the settlement of Watertown has ever been established, and it is probable that the migration of the families of the forty signers was a gradual one from Boston to the Watertown meadows, probably none among the forty signers of the articles being then actually in residence upon the site. The Rev. George Phillips was the minister appointed to the Watertown congregation, which for fully twenty years remained the largest and most important of all the Massachusetts church organizations. On September 17 (7th by old style), 1630, the Court of Assistants, sitting in the Great House at Charlestown passed resolution "That Treamountain shall be Boston; Mattapan, Dorchester; and ye town up ye Charles River, Watertown."

On November 30, 1630, the Court of Assistants assessed for the incomes of the two ministers then active; Mr. Wilson of Charlestown and Mr. Phillips in Watertown, upon the following basis—a total of £60, divided equally between them, and imposed as follows—£20 to Boston, £20 to Watertown, £10 to Charlestown, £6 to Roxbury, £3 to Medford, and £1 to Winnisimmet (Saugus & Revere). It would seem to be probable that this assessment was based upon an estimated proportionate balance among the churchmen in these several groups at that same time. In 1651 we were told by an early chronicler that Watertown had one hundred and sixty families, and that the town was largely agricultural in interest.

Watertown originally included Waltham, Weston, a large part of Lincoln, part of Sudbury, Wayland, part of Belmont, and New Towne (Cambridge) east of Mount Auburn cemetery; a large and rich agricultural area, and one still containing much rich archi-

Courtesy The Society for the Preservation of New England Antiquities

Photograph made in 1934, before restoration

ABRAHAM BROWNE HOUSE—1663—562 MAIN STREET, WATERTOWN, MASSACHUSETTS

This house illustrates the essentially English half-timber construction of the architecture of the early colonies

Room on First Floor

ABRAHAM BROWNE HOUSE—1663—562 MAIN STREET, WATERTOWN, MASSACHUSETTS

tectural material, although most of the actual early buildings have disappeared because of the wealth, prosperity, and business growth of the many important towns now within this same area, as well as the quickly acquired wealth of the prosperous owners of the old structures themselves.

The oldest house still standing within this area is the Abraham Browne House, in Watertown, near the further Waltham line. A few years ago this structure

what then became an interior partition—and forgotten. Hence it was that, when the restoration was started, two original three-part casement frames were uncovered, the first that actually had been found in place up to that time in New England. They were badly rotted, and portions were missing, but of certain things there could be no doubt.

An accompanying sketch indicates this frame and some details of its construction. Of the head and sill

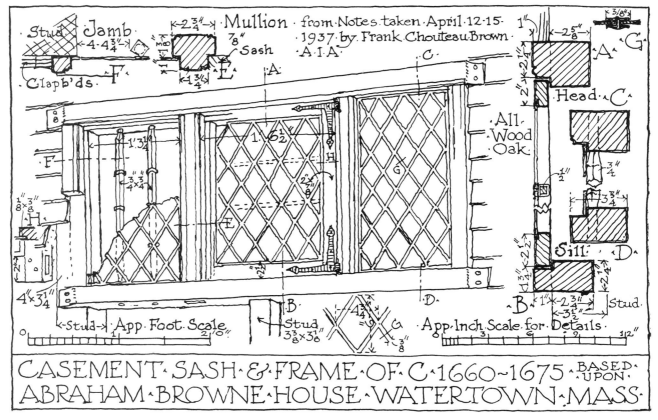

From fragments and sashes preserved by the Essex Institute and the Society for the Preservation of New England Antiquities, sash dimensions and "quarrel" (glass) sizes have been compiled. The lead "cames" are all of 3/8 th inch face width, nearly flat, except where lined or grooved from pressure applied when being fitted tight against the glass along their edges.

Name of House	Location	Date	Outside size wood sash	Size Glass Quarrel
Aptucxet Trading Post	Bourne	1627	unknown	4½" x 5½" high
Deacon Browne House	Salem	1654	20" x 29"	3½" x 4" high
Abraham Browne House	Watertown	1663	18½" x 26½"	4¾" x 6" high
Perkins House	Lynnfield	1670–75	14½" x 28½"	5¼" x 6¼" high
Ward House	Salem	1684	19" x 30"	4¾" x 5¾" high
Forbes House	Bridgewater	?	18½" x 20"	5⅛" x 6¾" high

was on the verge of demolition, but it was preserved and restored by the Society for the Preservation of New England Antiquities. The earliest portion was built in 1663, as a single house, having one room on each of two floors, with an attic in a steep roof above. It so remained until about 1730, when an addition was placed upon the northern side of the original house, with double hung windows—and the old casements on the north wall of the older portion were built into

pieces enough remained to make their sections and framing quite definite. The frame had no end jambs, using the upright studs for that purpose (F). The clapboards were nailed directly upon the upright studs, without exterior boarding. The intermediate mullions were clearly shown (E), but the moulding along the lower edge of the head—and the sides of the mullion —seems more like a shallow bead and fillet than the ogee used on the restoration. An upright stud coming in the middle of the space, framed into a notch in the back part of the crosspiece of the window frame on both top and bottom. The face treatment on the jamb was not found. It was evident it was narrow enough to allow the clapboards to stop against it and at the same time be nailed securely to the upright stud. The holes to receive the upright stiffening rods for the fixed leaded lights, and the mortices for the mullions, were clearly given.

filled or "daubed" with clay, and "limed" or surface-washed to prevent washing away by what water might work through the protecting wood wall covering. In this connection it might be recalled that the name of this type of wall covering came from "clay-boards"—so named because they were used to cover "clay walls" of houses. The manufacture and shipment of these clapboards back to England was a considerable business in New England from very early

ARTEMAS WARD, JR., HOUSE—1785—WESTON, MASSACHUSETTS

All this information has been assembled upon the accompanying sketch, along with some additional data as to sash and leading found in other locations. What dimensions it has been possible to assemble in regard to early casement sash sizes and glazing, have also been tabulated in the accompanying table. On the occasion of making replacement of the clapboards upon the south side of the old house a couple of years ago, Mr. Sumner Appleton secured a photograph of the exterior of the wall, with the clapboards removed, showing the half-timber framework and the brick nogging,

times. They were gotten out usually to 4' 0" lengths, ½" thick on the heavier edge, and thinned to ⅛" upon the other. They were six to eight inches wide, and the ends were beveled to lap over when laid. The best white pine was used and considerable skill was required to "rive out" the clapboards with the "frow" at the least lumber waste. The first mention of this product in New England was in Gov. Winthrop's journal, "Mr. Oldham had a small house near the weir at Watertown, made all of clapboards, burned August, 1632."

Porch Detail

Vestibule Detail

ARTEMAS WARD, JR., HOUSE—1785—WESTON, MASSACHUSETTS

BENNETT HOUSE—c1780—WAYLAND, MASSACHUSETTS

BEMIS HOUSE—1740—WALTHAM, MASSACHUSETTS

LAW OFFICE OF ARTEMAS WARD, JR., — 1785 — WESTON, MASSACHUSETTS

CALDWELL HOUSE — c1742 — WATERTOWN, MASSACHUSETTS

HAGAR HOUSE, WESTON, MASSACHUSETTS

BIGELOW HOUSE, WESTON, MASSACHUSETTS

This summarizes most of the definite information known of early wooden casement windows in eastern Massachusetts. They were used in houses built as late as 1720 or 1725, in the large coastal towns or cities—and probably for another ten or twenty years in the more remote inland communities; while the newer Georgian double-hung sash were gradually coming into use in different localities beginning about 1705 or 1710 and continuing over later years.

To pass from the seventeenth-century Browne House to the later primness of the Governor Gore place is a matter only of a mile or more, and nearly a hundred and fifty years; but it is possible to find many examples representative of the years between, without going outside the confines of old Watertown—or, indeed, without straying far from the next few miles of the old highway, laid out along the trail of the earliest Indian travel, in what was long known as the Connecticut Path, which passes only a hundred rods or so in front of the Governor's Mansion.

You can follow the road from Waltham to Watertown, from there through Kendall Green and Weston, and so on to Wayland, and—if you wish to visit the old Wayside Inn—over the old four arch bridge, 1791, into Sudbury—or branch off on the Connecticut Path toward Hartford. Shortly after passing through Weston Center, the road passes—on its left—the Golden Ball Tavern, 1768, and on its right, the Artemas Ward, Jr., House, 1785; and his picturesque little Lawyers Office, built about 1785, almost across the way, nestling under an umbrageous and historic elm.

Legend has it that this charming little "houselet" was built for a firm of lawyers, who, after a few years practice together, agreed to disagree—and parted. One kept to the old office, while his partner signed a paper undertaking not to open any competitive establishment within the same township. This he did, maintaining strictly to the letter of his bond—and so one finds another little lawyer's office, dating from nearly 1800, a scant couple of miles further along the Path, being perhaps as far as ten to fifteen feet over the line into the adjoining township of Wayland. It would seem that lawyers were—well, shall we say, lawyers—even in those dear departed days!

For other examples covering these intervening periods, Waltham itself still preserves, one on each side of this very same roadway, and just before reaching the Browne House, a small gambrel cottage known as the Caldwell House, and the uncompromising squareness of the old Bemis Homestead, across the road.

The Governor Christopher Gore place, 1805–1806, on the border marches between Waltham and Watertown, has been rescued recently from a double score of years of gradual disintegration, both moral and physical. Some twenty-five or so years ago, it was willed to the Episcopal Diocese of Boston, to be the site of a long-projected Episcopal Cathedral. After more years of anxious waiting, it was sold, and passed by turns rapidly through the hands of real estate agents, legal officials and factors; became the office building of an automobile manufactory, and an airplane plant; was a country club and a golf house—and just as it was about to be demolished to turn the deer park into more remunerative small house lots, its plight was recognized, and a few energetic individuals and societies banded themselves together to preserve the house and what remained of its former dependencies.

Unfortunately, since one Saturday a quarter-century ago, when the Boston Architectural Club made the unusual old dwelling and its grounds an excuse for a summer outing, or Field Day (the occasion—by the way—on which the principal early set of pictures of the house was taken) many changes have been made by transitory and passing tenants. The old balustrade about the roof has fallen, or been removed—as has also the gray and white paint that was lying in many coats over its old walls of small and pink brick, laid closely in Flemish fashion. The old garden and brick greenhouses have been obliterated; quaint coal grates; silver hardware and bronze fixtures, with crystal chandeliers, have vanished—along with truly mediaeval hooded tubs and curious early plumbing equipment, the silk velour curtains, dashing sleighs, and the orange-colored coach, in which, gay with flashing harness and liveried coachmen, footmen and outriders, the Governor used to make his imposing progress, from mansion to State House, and then home again!

The type of so-called Southern plan—with lower wings and end pavilions supporting each side of the central two story mansion—has only a few counterparts in New England; two in eastern Rhode Island, at Poppasquash and Portsmouth—and at least one other in Massachusetts. In the case of Gore Place, this Southern expansiveness of plan is accompanied by a most incongruous, if characteristically New England, paucity and reticence of detail, which, now the eaves balustrades are lacking, establishes an almost Puritanical rigor and baldness of aspect.

Yet, despite the ravishment of its parts, accessories, and furnishings; the substitution of some heavy later mantels for more delicate originals, Gore Place well repays a visit by its fine flavor of a vanished graciousness of living—such as is delicately expressed in the pure and flowing lines and fine sweep of the curving stairway—that can have had only too few enduring expositions in the grim business of living according to the dictates of religion and a Puritan conscience, in old-time New England!

North Elevation
GOVERNOR CHRISTOPHER GORE HOUSE—1805–1806—WATERTOWN, MASSACHUSETTS

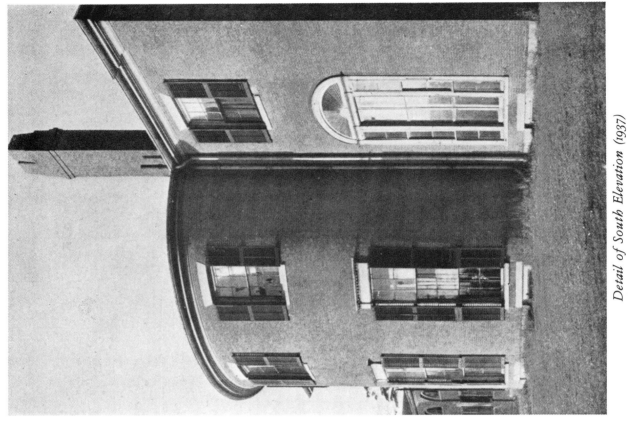

Detail of South Elevation (1937)

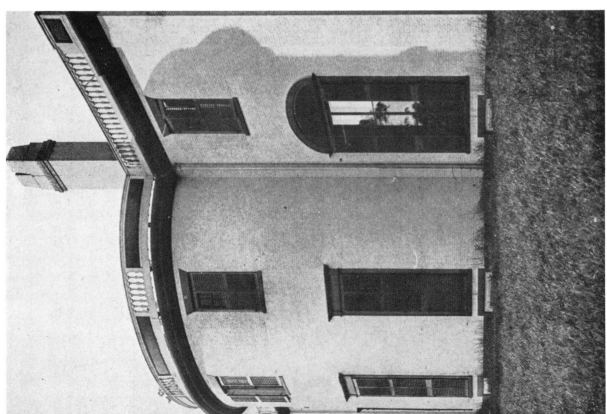

Detail of South Elevation (1912)

GOVERNOR CHRISTOPHER GORE HOUSE — 1805–1806 — WATERTOWN, MASSACHUSETTS

South Elevation

GOVERNOR CHRISTOPHER GORE HOUSE — 1805–1806 — WATERTOWN, MASSACHUSETTS

Stairway

Mantel Detail

GOVERNOR CHRISTOPHER GORE HOUSE—1805-1806—WATERTOWN, MASSACHUSETTS

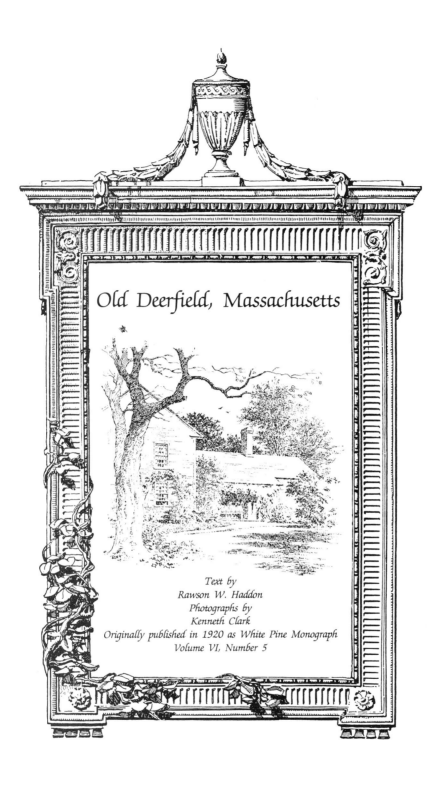

Old Deerfield, Massachusetts

Text by
Rawson W. Haddon
Photographs by
Kenneth Clark

Originally published in 1920 as White Pine Monograph
Volume VI, Number 5

MILLER HOUSE — c1710 — DEERFIELD, MASSACHUSETTS

OLD DEERFIELD, MASSACHUSETTS

I HOPE I shall be excused for mentioning the following bit of gossip which may seem to you to be but slightly connected with the strictest interpretation of my duty (for the present moment) as the introducer of the town of Deerfield, Massachusetts.

There was once a dignified old gentleman, who like that other old gentleman in *Cranford,* was noted all through a certain provincial town for always saying *just* the proper thing at the proper time. Imagine, therefore, the horror of his friends, and especially of his wife, when in the course of talk one evening, it having been discovered that a certain young man in the company was a bachelor, the old gentleman, turning to him in a most cordial and enthusiastic way, said, "God bless you, sir; you are indeed a fortunate man, and—" "What!" said his horrified wife. "How can you say such a thing, sir? HOW CAN YOU?" "You interrupt me, ma'am," was the old gentleman's reply. "What I was saying was, that he is a very fortunate man, because he has great happiness to look forward to."

The only excuse that I can give you for having mentioned this at all is that it gives me some slight precedent for suggesting to you that if you have not been to Deerfield you also are a fortunate man in that you still have to experience the great pleasure of your first trip through the "pleasant streets of that dear old town."

Starting at one end of Deerfield's main street, following it to its opposite end, and continuing then to the outlying districts, you will pass few houses that are not of interest either because of some historical association or for the unusual merit of their architectural design.

For all practical purposes each colonial town in New England repeats to a large degree in its general outlines the salient characteristics of every other colonial town. And with the exception of some few idiosyncrasies common to certain localities (as the difference between Massachusetts and Rhode Island house planning), the individuality that distinguishes Salem under the influence of McIntire or Greenfield during the era of Asher Benjamin, does not appear until the very end of the eighteenth or the beginning of the nineteenth century.

In Deerfield no predominating style exists to the extent that it does, for instance, in Salem. The buildings, all of which are good examples of their particular time, extend over the whole possible range of periods from the earliest Jacobean-like work through the Asher Benjamin phase to (it must unfortunately be acknowledged in one instance) the days when Egyptian-Moorish and in another instance Pre-Raphaelite Gothic were the proper thing in the vocabulary of the "genteel and up-to-date."

Of the hundred-odd houses in the town, the majority are of such great interest that this comparatively small philistine element will be wholly negligible in your enjoyment of this—as some of the natives boast—"sleepiest of all New England towns."

Exteriorly, as might be expected, the earliest houses here, as elsewhere, have little to show (excepting to the most enthusiastic of archaeological experts) that is of interest as architectural detail.

The interest in the earliest houses lies for the most part in their splendid outline and in the carefully studied proportioning of window and door opening to the solid mass of plain wall surfaces. And, as a rule, the detail which is found in connection with very early houses, when there is such detail as possesses distinctly architectural character, is an addition of later date than the building itself.

But whether this apparent sense of proportion was instinctive or purely accidental and governed, as may well have been the case, by structural exigencies into which no element of selection or proportioning was introduced by the builder, the result is none the less interesting and worthy of painstaking study by the architect of the present.

It is one of those facts which, like election-

the Old Manse, though competitors as to point of age are found in the Williams, Wetherald, and other houses.

The Williams House offers a number of problems, over the solution of which the inveterate expert might spend a large amount of time. As it stands today, the house may either be one built in 1707 to replace an earlier house which was erected by the town for Parson Williams and was burned in 1704, or it is possible that the 1707 house was destroyed and the present one erected in 1756 by the parson's son. Judged

PARSON WILLIAMS HOUSE, DEERFIELD, MASSACHUSETTS

Now Deerfield Academy, preserved in its present condition with unusual completeness. The best type of work of the middle of the eighteenth century.

time orators, "need no preliminary introduction here," that Colonial architecture possesses little or no monumentality, and its chief power must be said to lie in its characteristic grouping and the ornamental treatments of certain single details of building. It was only in the middle period, starting at perhaps the 1740's or 1750's in New England, that a definitely architectural manner began to assert itself in interior and exterior finish and design.

Perhaps the most interesting earlier example of this later manner in Deerfield is found in

in the light of its condition as it stands today, one would not hesitate, in spite of all local traditions, to assign to it the later date.

The plan, for instance, very emphatically contradicts the assumption of its early erection. A house in Massachusetts built in 1707 would, of course, have had a central chimney stack, with the rooms and entry grouped around it. The central chimney, however, does not appear in the house at the present time, and the fireplaces are at the central axis of the rear wall of the front rooms on each side of the hall.

FRARY HOUSE, DEERFIELD, MASSACHUSETTS

Part of the building was erected in 1683 and is the oldest house in the town.

The entrance door and frame, the window frames and the interior paneling and staircase also suggest the work of the middle rather than the early years of the century.

In spite of all this, however, the solution seems to be that here, as in other authenticated instances in the town, the house was changed and such additions made from time to time as were suggested and made possible by the prosperity of successive owners. Instances are not unknown in Deerfield in which the central chimney was removed at an early date and the plan and interior and exterior details so rearranged as to suggest a middle eighteenth-century erection.

Undoubtedly as it stands today, the Williams House consists of the original 1707 frame with improvements in plan and ornamental detail in the taste of the year 1756. It is known that at that date the parson's son, Elijah, "made certain marked alterations in the house, both external and internal," and probably left the building in substantially its present condition.

Richard B. Derby, in his chapter on the "Early Houses of the Connecticut River Valley," Volume V, Chapter 16 (in which, by the way, he has deprived the present number of some of its best thunder by anticipating it in the publication of the charming Asher Benjamin-like Horatio Hoyt House, and others), suggests in the instance of the doorway of the Williams House, and the same thing would hold good for the window frames, a date "probably several decades later" than 1756.

Whatever may be its date, the house is certainly of unusual interest. The scheme of fenestration and the broad blank space between the door and windows on the first floor, and the compact spacing of the windows themselves, are noteworthy features which must be taken into consideration in solving the problem of the remarkable appearance of solidity which the house presents.

The Miller House, built in 1710, which has three windows across the front on the second floor and two on the side (an unusual feature in early houses), might also be found after careful examination to be, in its present condition, the result of several additions. The house was built to replace an earlier one which was destroyed during the French and Indian War.

It will be remembered that Asher Benjamin lived and did some of his best work in Greenfield, a few miles distant from Deerfield. Undoubtedly careful investigation would uncover some hitherto unrecorded work by him in Deerfield. The doorway of the Bishop Porter House, a building that was erected in 1803, is most suggestive of his manner of design and is without doubt one of the most charming things of its sort in New England, as is also the doorway of the Hawkes House—which doorway has been used several times as a prototype, most successfully perhaps in connection with the restoration of a house dating from the Revolutionary period at Westport, Connecticut.

Front Door Detail
BISHOP PORTER HOUSE—1803—
DEERFIELD, MASSACHUSETTS

Front Door Detail
OLD MANSE — 1768 — DEERFIELD, MASSACHUSETTS
An unusually complete example of the type. It still
retains the original door, boot scrapers and knocker.

OLD MANSE—1768—DEERFIELD, MASSACHUSETTS
A typical example of the work of the middle—and historically Colonial—type.

WETHERALD HOUSE — 1752 — DEERFIELD, MASSACHUSETTS

A less elaborate example than the Williams House of the earliest "architectural" type. Just the sort of house that witches might choose for disturbances, via the chimney route, but for the lamentable fact that the chimney has been torn out, giving the house thereby a decidedly bald and unfinished appearance.

Front Door Detail

Side Door Detail

HAWKES HOUSE—1743—DEERFIELD, MASSACHUSETTS

Front Door Detail
ROOT HOUSE, DEERFIELD, MASSACHUSETTS

Front Door Detail
SMITH HOUSE, DEERFIELD, MASSACHUSETTS

There are earlier doorways, of course, and later ones, and earlier and later houses, and many local traditions and histories relating both to the houses and the people who lived in them, any one of which could be discussed at great length.

Taken all in all, Deerfield cannot be said to have any outstanding features of great monumentality, but it shows as clearly as perhaps any

which came with the later periods, and some of these examples, as the illustrations will show, are of more than usual interest, and many of them, as, for instance, the Old Manse House, are of considerable importance. Those parts of the Indian House which are preserved, namely, an interesting batten doorway, and two brackets which were originally over the overhang, and an interesting corner cupboard, are of unusual

STEBBINS HOUSE — c1772 — DEERFIELD, MASSACHUSETTS

A good example of the embarrassing frequence with which the visitor is confronted with houses that arouse his enthusiasm. Obviously, every house cannot be the "finest" or "most charming" and yet that seems to be what each one is. This particular house probably arouses more futile covetousness on the part of the architecturally inclined visitors than any other building in the town.

town of even larger size and greater importance could do, the complete evolution of architectural design from the earliest colonial period to the later and more self-conscious design of the early nineteenth century.

Examples of the earliest period are lacking, excepting for a few fragments of the so-called Indian House, dating from considerably before the Indian War, which are preserved by the local historical society in its museum. There are examples of each of the successive developments

consequence. The contour of these brackets is particularly good.

It is easy to understand how tenaciously the builders of the earliest houses would have clung to the traditions of building that were common in the parts of England in which they had received their earliest training. It is interesting to follow the changes which took place as time went on in the design of the buildings. As these builders dropped out, the work was carried out by their apprentices and by the apprentices of these apprentices. There are also examples that show the tendency, as time went on and the settlers became more prosperous, to adopt the styles and manners of living that were found at that time in England. This change, however, does not show the work that was indigenous to the localities from which the builders came, but reflects, as nearly as changed conditions would allow, the latest style in design, and, for that matter, in every other detail of living.

During and shortly after the Revolution a new influence was introduced by the publication in America of reprints of English books on architecture, and at a later period by the books of Asher Benjamin.

Regarding the translation of a manner of building which is essentially one of brick and stone into the easily obtainable white pine and other local woods, Joy Wheeler Dow has this to say in his *American Renaissance*.

"The predominant local color which distinguishes American Renaissance has been given to it by what has been our great national building commodity, *i.e.*, wood. The Greeks and Romans built of stone when they had the money to pay for it. Both stone and wood have grain, and have to be used with the same careful regard for it. Whether we build our columns up of stone or wooden sections—latitudinal in the one case, longitudinal in the other—to support a cornice also constructed in sections according to the convenient sizes of commerce for the particular material, makes no difference to the canons of art so long as we are not trying to deceive or to imitate one material with another simply with that end in

view. It is extremely doubtful if our American ancestors were ever guilty of premeditated deception. Their material was an honest material, it had to be fashioned in some way; why not after the manner of the Renaissance?"

Sir Christopher Wren being the supreme actor upon the architectural stage in England at that time, it is natural that his influence would be strongly felt in the transplantation of architectural ideas between the two countries.

The earliest examples of Renaissance in Deerfield were not always accurate renderings of classic traditions in their design or construction, but there is a certain sturdiness and self-reliance shown in this work which speaks well for the mentalities of the men who were responsible for the work. The translation of details, which were primarily adopted for construction in stone, being built of wood, was carried out more often than not with an apparently large amount of skill, that after all makes the thing seem all right.

Side Door Detail

STEBBINS HOUSE, DEERFIELD, MASSACHUSETTS

Though less elaborate than the front door
it shows remarkable consistence in design.

Attention cannot be called too often to the fact that American work does not show a real independence in design until the early years of the nineteenth century. Such men as McIntire, Hoadley, McComb and others not only contributed very largely to the development of architectural design in America; theirs was a very definite and valuable contribution to the total of the architectural history of the nineteenth century. In Deerfield there are examples not only of the earlier periods which show English influence but also some most excellent examples of this later work of American inspiration.

Front Door Detail
STEBBINS HOUSE, DEERFIELD, MASSACHUSETTS

The front door of the Stebbins House is certainly a word to the wise, and ought to tell as much as could be put into whole volumes about "White Pine, and Where to Use It." Built one hundred and forty-eight years ago, the wood is as sound and the detail as crisp and distinct as it was in 1772 when the builder put it into place.

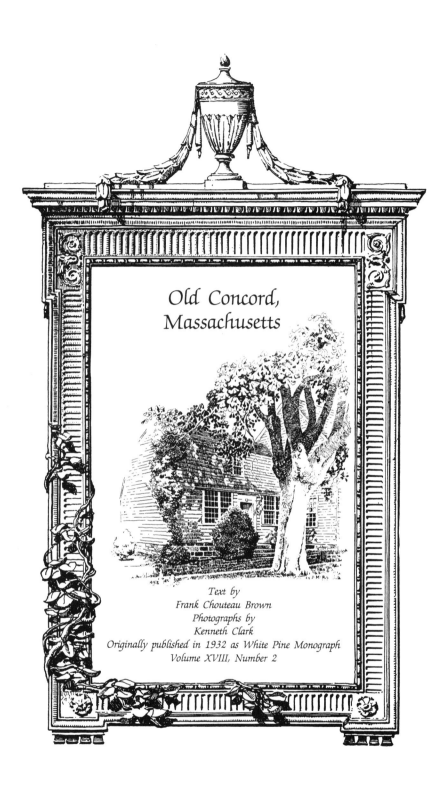

Old Concord, Massachusetts

Text by
Frank Chouteau Brown
Photographs by
Kenneth Clark

Originally published in 1932 as White Pine Monograph
Volume XVIII, Number 2

PENNIMAN-STEARNS HOUSE, BEDFORD, MASSACHUSETTS
Reuben Duren, Architect

OLD CONCORD, MASSACHUSETTS

THE Pilgrims landed at Plymouth Rock in 1620. Nine years later Charles the First signed the Charter of Massachusetts, and a year after, in 1630, nearly fifteen hundred men and women arrived under Winthrop and Dudley to settle upon its eastern shores. In that year, the city of Boston was settled and Watertown and Cambridge also founded.

The first inland settlement in Massachusetts was made in 1635, although it is said that it had been planned in England two years earlier; and this seems plausible from the fact that all the earliest people to settle on the site of Concord village came directly from England, and originally its only neighbors for years were New Towne — later Cambridge — and Watertown.

The General Court of Massachusetts issued an act of incorporation on September 2nd, 1635, for the area then known as Musketaquid, from its Indian name, proclaiming that it "shall hereafter be called Concord." And Gov. Winthrop stated his grant was made to "Mr. Buckly and . . . , merchant, and about twelve more families, to begin a town." The two principal incorporators were undoubtedly the Rev. Peter Bulkeley and Maj. Simon Willard; and it was placed to include the Great Fields or Great Meadows, along the banks of the Concord River, located to the north of the Boston Road, which were immediately realized as being especially fertile.

The original area was increased by other grants. In November, 1637, the Court gave to Gov. Winthrop and his lieutenant deputy, Mr. Thomas Dudley, large additional lands bounding on the Concord River. In June, 1641, Shawshen was granted to Cambridge; and on September 23rd, 1729, Bedford, with its sister town of Westford, were incorporated as the twenty-fifth and twenty-sixth of the fifty-nine townships finally set up in Middlesex County; Bedford's area being largely taken from Concord and Billerica — also including the whole of the area granted to Winthrop and part of the Shawshen or Shawshine grant, upon which the first dwelling had been built in 1642, and called Shawshen House. Subsequently, both Lincoln, 1754, and Carlisle, 1757, were set off from Concord; while from Bedford, Acton was set off in 1684, and incorporated in 1735, Stow in 1670, and Littleton in 1715, these various townships being made up out of sections of the earliest inland townland, and new sections adjoining it.

John Duren, of the first generation in this country, settled in Billerica, possibly as early as 1659, and Reuben Duren or Durrant (the name being also spelled in other ways) was of the fourth generation. He married Mary Gould of Chelmsford on Jan. 11th, 1770, and died on Jan. 4th, 1821. He was known as "an architect and builder of first-class dwelling houses of the town" and those for Col. Timothy Jones and Rev. Mr. Penniman (now the Stearns House), pages 102 and 113, are examples — the latter being perhaps his second house in that vicinity. The Rev. Samuel Stearns was ordained on April 27th, 1796, at which time the house for his predecessor, the third minister, was not entirely finished.

In 1792 Reuben Duren purchased a tavern in Billerica, which he kept till he removed to New Ipswich, New Hampshire, where he later became famed as a builder of meeting houses. His reputation as bridge builder, earned in Bedford, was enhanced by his model for a bridge over the Merrimac at Pawtucket Falls, which was given precedence over many competitors.

The Hildreth House at Concord, set off from all present main traveled roads, and facing out upon a quiet little triangle of green, preserves something of its original flavor of quiet dignity and comparative isolation. It would appear of about the same date as the Stearns House at Bedford from similarities of detail; the almost direct repetition of idea shown in the two doorways; the general proportions and composition of both façades indicating, with other internal evidence, that the legend that the Hildreth House had been produced by the same designer as the Stearns dwelling is probably correct. The interiors, shown upon the measured drawing of the section, express something of the restraint, almost the inarticulateness, of many of the early New Englanders when attempting to work in the more sumptuous, freely flowing manner that seems to have come so easily to many of their contemporaries — or even to designers of somewhat earlier times — in the southern colonies.

Deane Winthrop, a son of the Governor, was among those who signed the petition for the setting up of a part of the inland area as the township of Groton. In 1655 two new townships were authorized, Shawshin and Groton. The date of "Groton plantations" is fairly well established as between May 23 or 29, 1655.

When the line between New Hampshire and Massachusetts was surveyed and located in 1741, it was disclosed that Groton had lost to New Hampshire a large part of its area, so that there was a Groton in each state up to January 1st, 1837, when the name of Nashua was given to that portion in New Hampshire.

Other portions of Groton went to make the new Pepperell, set off November 26th, 1742, but not signed by Gov. Shirley until April 12th, 1753. This new township was named after Sir William Pepperell. Shirley was set off as a district January 5th, 1753, but did not become a separate township until August 23rd, 1775. Ayer was incorporated from portions of Groton and Shirley; about half of the town of Dunstable came from Groton lands, and the full tale is told with the mention that smaller parts of Groton were taken for Harvard, Littleton, and Westwood in Massachusetts, and Nashua and Hollis in New Hampshire. These several partitions left Groton finally with an area of less than half of its original forty thousand acres.

One of the older small schools in Massachusetts was in Groton, known as the Academy, and later as Lawrence Academy, in honor of the several benefits conferred upon it by both Amos and William Lawrence of Medford, Massachusetts. Amos Lawrence had been born and educated in Groton, and had besides served an apprenticeship for seven years in the old store of James Brazer in Groton, up to April 22nd, 1807. James Brazer was originally one of the founders of the Academy, subscribing £15 to the building fund in 1792; and so it was rather appropriate for Amos Lawrence to purchase James Brazer's House, built about 1802, and situated immediately south of and adjacent to the Academy property, and give it to the Academy in 1848. The estate of Judge Samuel Dana had been added to the Academy property in 1836; and so these two representative New England dwellings have been fortunately preserved until today, side by side upon the main road, facing out across the Meadows, being used as dormitories for the Academy scholars. During his later lifetime Samuel Dana served his district as representative in Congress, he had been president of the Massachusetts Senate, and had also served the town of Groton as its first postmaster (1801–1804).

The visitor driving through the main street of Groton today can still capture something of the village charm, from its few principal dwellings grouped closely together, with the two most imposing mansions side by side upon the higher ground that formerly looked off over the meadow farms and fields. Another fact of interest, but of no particular architectural value, except that it keys into the family record of another beautiful Colonial mansion located nearby in Woburn, relates to Loammi Baldwin, Jr., a son of the distinguished engineer of that name, who was studying law in Groton in January, 1802, when the predecessor of the Brazer House burned. Young Baldwin was boarding with Dr. Oliver Prescott, Sr., of the same family as William Prescott, who came from Groton and commanded the American forces at the Battle of

Bunker Hill. He witnessed this fire and was so impressed by it, and the inefficiency of the methods then employed to fight it, that he undertook to construct an "engine" in an old shop located where the William Bruce drugstore was toward the end of the last century. This engine, known as Torrent No. 1, was used for years in Groton, and was working in West Groton, as late as 1890, the only piece of apparatus then available in that village for the fighting of fire.

Shirley Center, the oldest section of the present township of that name, remains still largely undisturbed, partly because of its isolated position, having been left at one side when the newer automobile highway was routed through that area. It is undoubtedly for that reason that it is still possible to get much the effect of that little center of colonial life when visiting the dwelling of Thomas Whitney, son of the Rev. Phineas Whitney, the first minister of Shirley, after its being set apart as a separate township. This occurred in 1753, on January 5th; the first meeting house having been built in 1754. It was replaced by a second and larger structure in 1773. The cupola, shown on page 116, was probably a part of this original building. Unfortunately, porches were added in 1804, along with other changes, and the structure was again remodeled in 1839; so that it is no longer possible to get an interesting photograph of the entire building.

Mr. Thomas Whitney, whose house remains the most important of the small group around the village, was born March 19th, 1771, and died on January 14th, 1844. We have the date of his marriage to Henrietta Parker, which was July 7th, 1799; and it is probable that his hospitable farmhouse was rebuilt a little while after that date. Standing a little back from the main street, behind its guardian elms, it is an able representative of the four-square New England type that came into being shortly before the Revolution and persisted until the more daintily graceful structures of the 1815 to 1830 period succeeded it, just before the turn to the heavy dignity of the Neo-Greek influence was to flow over the country; replacing these gracious homes with Greek temples, somewhat arbitrarily and awkwardly made to serve the purposes of a family dwelling.

The front of the house facing the Common still shows the old type shutters, lacking the middle cross style. The detail of the front porch indicates a period preceding the date of Thomas Whitney's marriage, to which some of the enlargement and additions might easily belong. The generous spacing of the front entrance porch columns, their slight, almost crude, entasis, the heavy molding of necking and base, all point to workmanship of a time much nearer the Revolution, or even somewhat preceding.

Detail of Façade
JAMES BRAZER HOUSE, GROTON, MASSACHUSETTS

JAMES BRAZER HOUSE, GROTON, MASSACHUSETTS

SAMUEL DANA HOUSE, GROTON, MASSACHUSETTS

Side Entrance
SAMUEL DANA HOUSE, GROTON, MASSACHUSETTS

TYPICAL HOUSES ALONG MAIN STREET, GROTON, MASSACHUSETTS

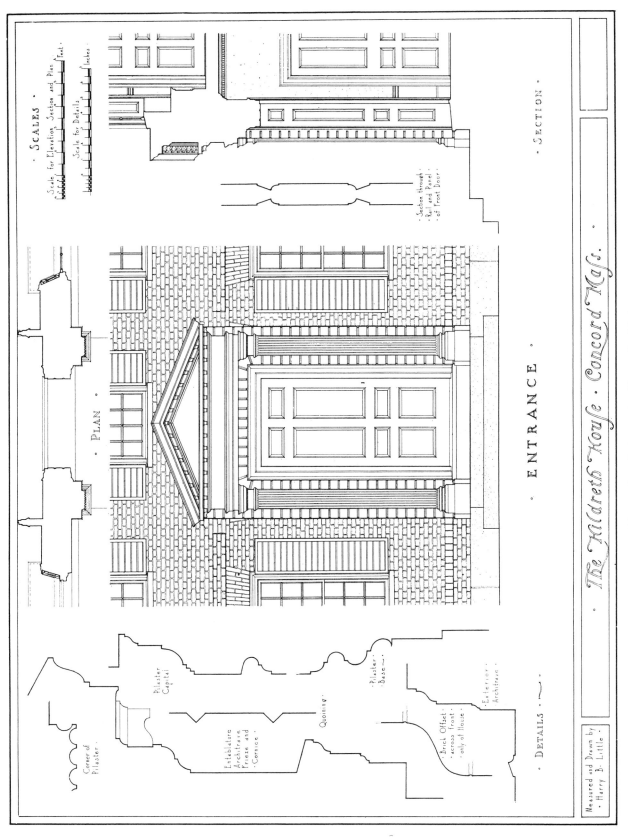

· SCALES ·

· Scale for Elevation Section and Plan ·

· Scale for Details ·

· PLAN ·

· SECTION ·

· Section through · Rail and Panel · of Front Door ·

· ENTRANCE ·

· DETAILS · ~

· Corner of · Pilaster ·

· Pilaster · Capital ·

· Entablature · Architrave · Frieze and · Cornice ·

· Quoining ·

· Pilaster · Base ·

· Brick Offset · across front · only of House ·

· Exterior · Architrave ·

Measured and Drawn by · Harry B. Little ·

· The Hildreth House · Concord Mass. ·

Measured and drawn by Harry B. Little

HILDRETH HOUSE, CONCORD, MASSACHUSETTS

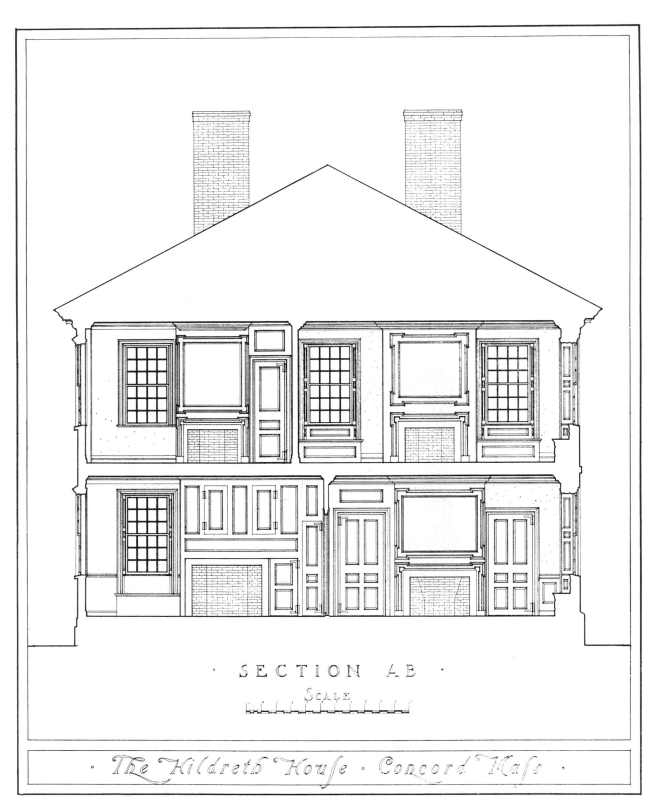

· S E C T I O N · A·B ·

S<small>CALE</small>

· The Hildreth House · Concord Mass ·

Measured and drawn by Harry B. Little

Doorway
PENNIMAN-STEARNS HOUSE, BEDFORD, MASSACHUSETTS
Reuben Duren, Architect

SIDE AND FRONT DOORWAYS — THOMAS WHITNEY HOUSE, SHIRLEY CENTER, MASSACHUSETTS

THOMAS WHITNEY HOUSE, SHIRLEY CENTER, MASSACHUSETTS

Cupola
MEETING HOUSE, SHIRLEY CENTER, MASSACHUSETTS

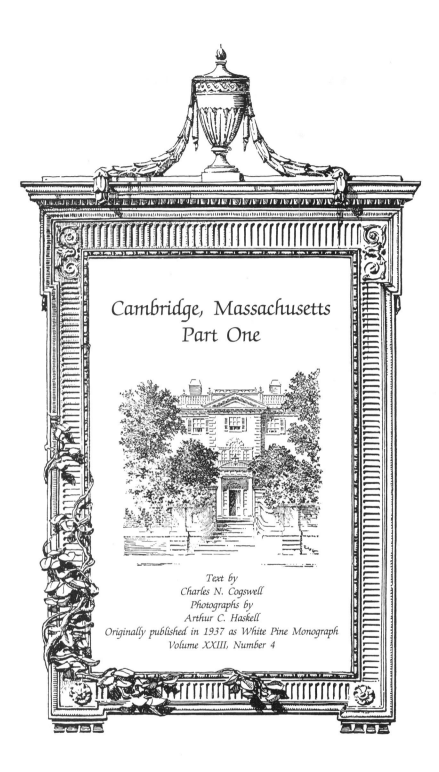

Cambridge, Massachusetts
Part One

Text by
Charles N. Cogswell
Photographs by
Arthur C. Haskell
Originally published in 1937 as White Pine Monograph
Volume XXIII, Number 4

JUDGE JOSEPH LEE-NICHOLS HOUSE, 159 BRATTLE STREET, CAMBRIDGE
Built about 1660, remodeled about 1760

CAMBRIDGE, MASSACHUSETTS, PART ONE

THE present city of Cambridge had its origin when a part of the area between Charlestown and Watertown was selected as a "fit place for a fortified town" in December of 1630, by the colonists then settling at Boston and Charlestown. It was also agreed that the officers and assistants would all build dwellings there during the following year. But by the end of 1631 only Dep. Gov. Thomas Dudley and Simon Bradstreet had actually built; and Gov. Dudley had his home taken down and re-erected in Boston.

Nevertheless, on February 3, 1631–1632, the Governor and assistants ordered "that there should be three scoore pounds levyed out of the several plantations within the lymitts of this pattent toward the makeing of a pallysadoe aboute the newe towne" — and it was as Newe Towne that Cambridge was known until May 2, 1638, when the change of name was authorized. This levy was distributed as follows: "Watertown, viii £.; the Newe Towne, iii £.; Charlton, vii £.; Meadford, iii £.; Saugus & Marble Harbor, vi £.; Salem, iv £. x s.; Boston viii £.; Rocksbury, vii £.; Dorchester, vii £.; Wessagusset, v £.; Winettsemet, xxx s." The enclosure was actually constructed, and surrounded by a "fosse," or ditch, beginning at Wind Mill Hill (now end of Ash Street) and continuing along the north side of the present Common, and then onwards to the river.

As the space between the two earlier settled towns appeared very limited to the new settlers, especially when the congregation of Thomas Hooker began to arrive, its area was enlarged in 1634 to include Brookline (Muddy River) — which was lost again when Mr. Hooker and his followers left for Hartford a few years later! Then Brighton and Newtown, across the river, Arlington (Menotomy) and most of what is now Lexington were added to the Cambridge area. Still later more land was taken from Billerica (Shawshine), parts of Bedford and Carlisle, and Tewksbury and Chelmsford.

In 1664 Newton established its own church, being finally separated in 1688. The Farms (Lexington) had secured its church in 1696, and was incorporated in 1713. Part of Watertown was annexed in 1754 and 1755, and, in 1802, part of Charlestown, now known as Somerville.

The growth of New Towne was very rapid. On March 29, 1631, forty-two people were listed as inhabitants, although these may have been only the names of the then established lot owners. One of the earliest references to any sort of building law in the new colonies is in a letter of Thomas Dudley's, in which he says "we have ordered that no man there shall build his chimney with wood nor cover his house with thatch." If this order was obeyed, these new structures were being built upon the most permanent basis then employed — which would be easily possible if their owners were living in Boston or Charlestown, and could row back and forth while the new buildings across the river were being constructed.

There was a ferry at about the present location of Brighton bridge; while a bridge and causeway across the marshes to the ferry landing was being planned at the south end of the present Dunster Street as early as December 7, 1635. But before that, in 1631, a canal was cut from the channel in the Charles River through the marshes to firm land near the center of the town settlement. It was 12 feet broad and 7 feet deep, and cost £30. This indicates the early importance of transportation by waterway in American settlements. Indeed, the entire Cambridge side of the river was marshy and low. The only embankment remaining from the fortifications built by the besieging American army during the Revolution, now preserved as a small park in Cambridge, was originally erected upon a knoll then surrounded by marshland.

At this early date, the river and marsh were part of a larger tidal basin that included the Cambridge and Charlestown banks, and, on the south, beyond Beacon Hill, water and marsh extended way across to Washington Street and as far west as the highlands of Roxbury. It further continued along the Brookline (then Muddy) River and the Newton banks of the Charles as well.

The two first ministers in Boston and Cambridge

were Mr. Cotton and Mr. Hooker. They were upon opposite sides in the then highly important Antinomian and Famalistic controversies. Matters came to such a pass that, in 1635 and 1636, most of the First Church congregation from Cambridge removed with their minister, Mr. Hooker, to Hartford, Connecticut. This exodus took away more than fifty families, and lost the town of Brookline to Cambridge, as it had been given only if Thomas Hooker and his following

lege on November 15, 1637, which was then ordered to be established at New Towne, and 2⅔ acres were set apart for that purpose, including the present sites of Holworthy, Stoughton, and Hollis Halls. On March 13, 1638–1639 it was named after John Harvard, who had in his will left the new college half his estate, £7000, and all his library—260 volumes.

Oldest among present Cambridge dwellings is the Cooper-Austin House, on Linnaean Street, which is

East Parlor Fireplace
COOPER-AUSTIN HOUSE—1657—CAMBRIDGE, MASSACHUSETTS

should remain! In fact, much of the continuous plea for more land during these first years was perhaps as much as anything to provide an excuse for the removal of this group. Though, if we allow for the large amount of swampland, and the already established limits of Charlestown (then including Somerville and East Cambridge) and Watertown (which then came to the nearer line of Mt. Auburn cemetery) there was not much usable land remaining, especially for the grazing of large herds of cattle and sheep that belonged to these first settlers, mostly concerned with farming.

Cambridge was adopted as the site of the new col-

owned by the Society for the Preservation of New England Antiquities and was built by Deacon John Cooper in 1657. In evidence, was his license from the town, given in that year "to fell timber on the Cow Common for his building." At that time, and for many years after, the Cow Common extended northward to this location. Linnaean Street, then Love Lane, was laid out in 1725. Beams and frame are of hewn oak, the timbered ceiling in the east parlor being one of the finest in the vicinity.

John Cooper was a selectman, town clerk, and deacon. In an inventory of the estate, taken in 1783, the

COOPER-AUSTIN HOUSE — 1657 — 21 LINNAEAN STREET, CAMBRIDGE, MASSACHUSETTS

house was valued at £100, and 11½ acres of land at £345. In 1807 the house passed into the Austin family, and repairs made at that time may have included the first story entrance vestibule. About 1820 a fire damaged the west side, and the earliest remaining room and fireplace is now at the right of the entrance.

Until within a few years, Cambridge has been fortunate in that its business district developed largely in the portions nearer Boston and the river; so that the

But first, we should notice two historic dwellings near Harvard Square. On Harvard Square is Wadsworth House, built for President Benjamin Wadsworth, in 1726, and used as the official dwelling of the presidents of the college for over a hundred years. It is still maintained for college purposes; and its main outlines—of roof gambrel, dormers, windows, and porches—have been carefully preserved. It was occupied for a short time as Washington's headquarters,

GENERAL WILLIAM BRATTLE HOUSE—1727—42 BRATTLE STREET, CAMBRIDGE, MASSACHUSETTS

part lying beyond Harvard Square, out as far as Mount Auburn cemetery, has remained a residential district, affected only by the expansion of the university. Consequently, there may still be seen, within less than a mile along Brattle Street, many imposing old dwellings that were known, before the Revolution, as Tory Row. So by ignoring intervening houses of more recent date, in the progress of a short walk one may see more important old houses—importance both architecturally as well as historically or from association with famous owners or occupants—than anywhere else so near a large city in all New England.

before his removal to the larger Longfellow House.

Another old building in this near vicinity is Apthorp House, sometimes known as The Bishop's Palace, which was built in 1761 by the Rev. East Apthorp, the first rector of Christ Church, when he married Elizabeth, niece of Gov. Hutchinson and granddaughter of Gov. Shirley. Following his graduation from Jesus College, Oxford, in 1759, he (a native of Boston) was appointed missionary to Cambridge and returned here by the Society for the Propagation of the Gospel in Foreign Parts. One of his sisters married Thomas Bulfinch, and was the mother of Charles Bulfinch.

"ELMWOOD"—1760—CAMBRIDGE, MASSACHUSETTS
Corner of Mt. Auburn Street and Elmwood Avenue

Mantel, Southwest Room, Second Floor

Mantel, Southwest Room, First Floor

"ELMWOOD" — 1760 — CORNER OF MT. AUBURN STREET AND ELMWOOD AVENUE, CAMBRIDGE, MASSACHUSETTS

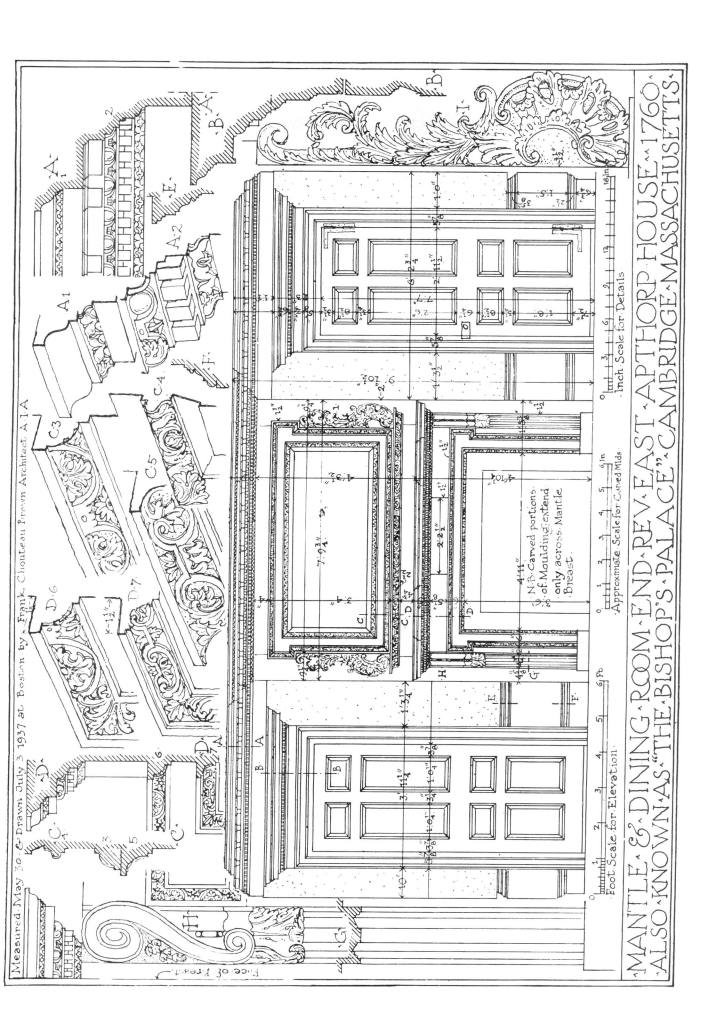

MANTLE & DINING ROOM END REV. EAST APTHORP HOUSE 1760.
ALSO KNOWN AS "THE BISHOP'S PALACE" CAMBRIDGE MASSACHUSETTS.

Measured May 30 & Drawn July 3 1937 at Boston by Frank Chouteau Brown Architect A1A

Inch Scale for Details

Approximate Scale for Carved Mlds

Foot Scale for Elevation

N.B. Carved portions of Moulding extend only across Mantle Breast.

Face of Tread

Detail of Mantel in Dining Room
APTHORP HOUSE—1761—15 PLYMPTON STREET, CAMBRIDGE, MASSACHUSETTS

APTHORP HOUSE—1761—15 PLYMPTON STREET, CAMBRIDGE, MASSACHUSETTS

The Rev. Apthorp's father, a wealthy merchant and pillar of King's Chapel, was also Commissary and Paymaster of the British forces in Boston. This background of wealth, education, and travel fully explains the outstanding elegance of the house he built, which remains conspicuous, even today.

The Rev. East Apthorp gave up his Cambridge ministry and went to England in 1764, his house being sold, in 1765, to John Borland, husband of Anna Vassall, for one thousand pounds. When Borland was forced to leave Cambridge, as a well known Tory, the property was confiscated and used by the Committee of Safety during the Revolution, at one time quartering three companies of troops. After Burgoyne's surrender at Saratoga, General William Heath wrote General Washington, "Gen. Burgoyne is in Mr. Borland's house, formerly Putnam's quarters, and the other principal officers in the town of Cambridge."

In 1784 the house was purchased by Jonathan Simpson, Jr., husband of Jane Borland, who repaired and occupied it, and at this time the upper story may have been added. Although, according to tradition, it was built for the slaves of John Borland, the rooms now are paneled in a style that would hardly justify that use — unless the slaves were lodged in the low upper attic, above the third floor. During this occupancy, both Linden and Plympton streets were laid out through the property to meet the real estate boom caused by the opening of the new bridge in 1793. Capt. Thomas Warland came into possession in 1803, and it remained in that family until 1897, when Randolph Hall, a college dormitory, was built on Bow Street, within the old box garden, a small part of which remains in the court yard between the two buildings.

The Brattle House, on Brattle Street, formerly had in its grounds to the east, the old Town Spring, which led into a pond, which had been parked and beautified until it was known as one of the show places of New England. The present dwelling was built by Gen. William Brattle, about 1727. It still retains a few of the paneled rooms, and a fine stairway with hand-carved balusters. The porch is — as usual — a later addition. Gen. Brattle was one of the richest men in Cambridge, and Major-General of all the province from 1771, an overseer at Harvard, and a well known Tory. The house was occupied by Major Thomas Mifflin, first *aide-de-camp* to General Washington, and Commissary-General during the siege of Boston.

For nearly half a century the house has been owned by the Cambridge Social Union, and has also become a community center for the Red Cross, etc.

Nearby, across the street from the Brattle House, is the Read House, probably built by James Read, who came from Kent, England, in 1725. In the southwest chamber is an inscription, traced on the wet plaster, which reads, "James Read, May 18, 1738." This house has been many times changed, but the garden between it and Brattle Street has been maintained now for many years, and certainly since 1866. The simple but unusual details of the entrance doorway are now upon the face of a vestibule, to which it was probably advanced from the main wall of the house at the time the vestibule was added.

Farther along on Brattle Street and facing Longfellow Park is the well known Vassall-Craigie-Longfellow House, the mecca of all visitors to Cambridge.

Built by Col. John Vassall, in 1759, this house was General Washington's headquarters in 1775. It was lived in by Dr. Andrew Craigie, 1793–1819, and he made additions to the house at the back. After Mrs. Craigie's death, in 1841, Henry Wadsworth Longfellow, who had occupied rooms in the house from 1837, in Mrs. Craigie's lifetime, became the owner in 1843. He died in 1882, and the estate continues in the possession of his descendants. Large and stately, with certain Victorian changes and its literary flavor, this house is one of the best specimens of Colonial architecture in Cambridge.

Half a mile beyond, at the corner of Kennedy Avenue, stands the Judge Joseph Lee-Nichols House, beautifully preserved and maintained by its present architect-owner. The house dates from about 1660, although the third story was probably a later addition. The rooms on either side of the front hall are twenty feet square.

Elmwood Avenue, leading off Brattle Street to the left, brings us to "Elmwood" — where lived for many years James Russell Lowell, the scholar and poet. In 1848, he thus described his first study at "Elmwood:" "Here I am in my garret. I slept here when I was a curly-headed boy, and in it I used to be shut up without a lamp — my mother saying none of her children should be afraid of the dark. It is a pleasant room facing — almost equally — towards the morning and the afternoon sun. In winter I can see the sunset, in summer I can see it only as it lights up the tall trunks of the English elms in front of the house, making them sometimes, when the sky behind them is lead-covered, seem of the most brilliant yellow. In winter, my view is a wide one, taking in a part of Boston. As the spring advances and one after the other of our trees puts forth, the landscape is cut off from me, piece by piece, till, by the end of May, I am closeted in a cool and rustic privacy of leaves. Then I begin to bud with the season, when I can sit at my open window and my friendly leaves hold their hands before my eyes to prevent their wandering to the landscape. I can sit down and write."

Detail of Porch
WADSWORTH HOUSE—1726—HARVARD SQUARE, CAMBRIDGE, MASSACHUSETTS

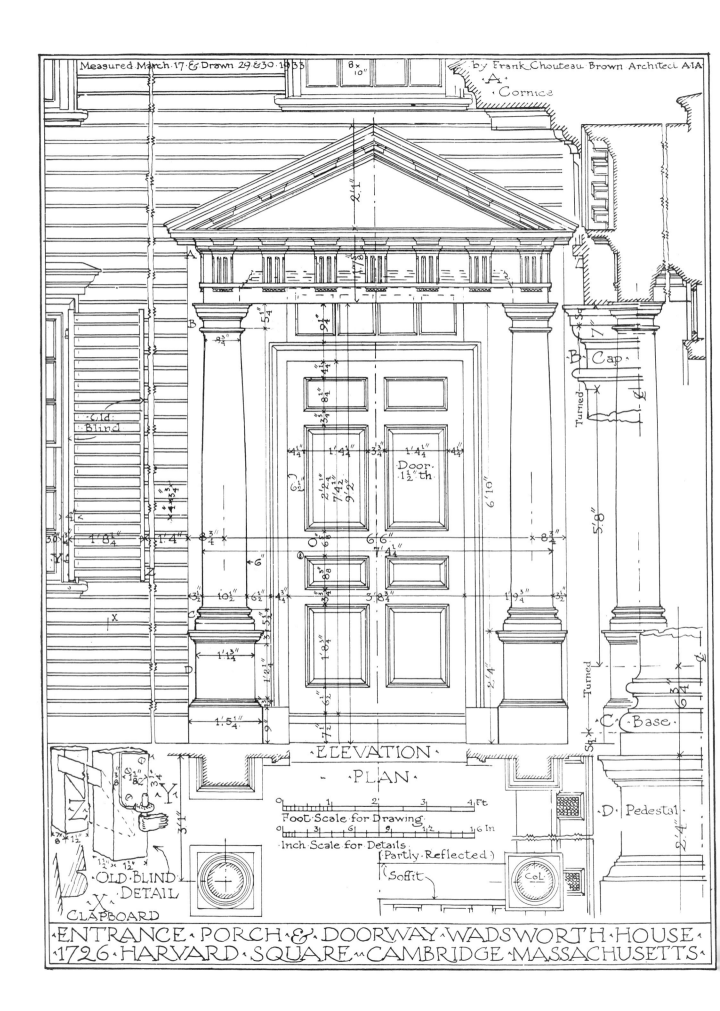

Measured March 17 & Drawn 29 & 30 1933

8 × 10"

by Frank Chouteau Brown Architect A.I.A.

·A· Cornice

·B· Cap

Old Blind

Door 1½" th.

·C· Base

·ELEVATION·

- PLAN -

OLD·BLIND DETAIL

CLAPBOARD

Col.

·D· Pedestal

0   1   2'   3   4 Ft
·Foot·Scale·for·Drawing·

0   3   6   9   1'2   16 In
·Inch·Scale·for·Details·

·(Partly·Reflected·)

Soffit

·ENTRANCE·PORCH·&·DOORWAY·WADSWORTH·HOUSE·
·1726·HARVARD·SQUARE·CAMBRIDGE·MASSACHUSETTS·

VASSALL-CRAIGIE-LONGFELLOW HOUSE — 1759 — 105 BRATTLE STREET, CAMBRIDGE, MASSACHUSETTS

Detail of Doorway
JAMES READ HOUSE—1725—55 BRATTLE STREET, CAMBRIDGE, MASSACHUSETTS

Cambridge, Massachusetts
Part Two

Text by
Charles N. Cogswell
Photographs by
Arthur C. Haskell
Originally published in 1937 as White Pine Monograph
Volume XXIII, Number 5

JOHN VASSALL HOUSE, 94 BRATTLE STREET, CAMBRIDGE, MASSACHUSETTS
Original West Front, on Hawthorn Street, Before 1686
Rear (East) Portion Added by Maj. Henry Vassall in 1746

CAMBRIDGE, MASSACHUSETTS, PART TWO

STARTING, as the settlement did, without formality; Cambridge — rather like Topsy — "just growed." And the rapidity of its growth was somewhat determined by its location between such early and important settlements as Charlestown and Watertown.

One of the earliest thoroughfares in the colony was the pathway connecting these two early townships. As we have seen in Chapter 5, Watertown was set up by men already living in Boston and Charlestown. They were able to construct their new dwellings in less haste, as they were already fairly well housed, but were removing to more open country so they might increase their livestock and take up farming more exclusively. Consequently, there must have been an unusual amount of travel along the northern bank of the Charles. Any Boston dweller would most easily ferry across the river, below the marshes, and then take the Charlestown road, cutting inland almost in a direct line to Watertown Square (as it is today), thus leaving all the marshland on the Cambridge bank of the river to his left. This pathway came later to be known as the King's Highway.

Leaving Charlestown, this road entered Cambridge over what is now Kirkland Street, crossed the Common near the Washington Elm, then through Mason and Brattle streets and Elmwood Avenue, where it passed the end of the lane leading down to the ferry to Brighton, and continued on to Watertown, Waltham, and across the river to Newtown. The first settlement of Cambridge was made between this roadway and the river, to the south of the Common, in the area now covered by the new college "houses" of the university — or, at least, so much of it as was then above water — and between the Charlestown and Watertown boundaries, which were less than a mile apart.

Of especial interest to architects should be the record of the "first house built in Cambridge," as well as a word about its first owner. As early as March 10, 1628–1629, the Massachusetts Bay Company in England agreed with one Thomas Graves, an "engineer" of Gravesend, to go to New England and lay out the town of Charlestown. Graves arrived in Salem, early in July, 1629, with Higginson. He went at once to Charlestown, laid out its plan, and directed the building of the palisade, and its Great House. As part of his agreed recompense he was given one hundred acres of land, located in what is now East Cambridge but was then Charlestown; for, on March 6, 1632, we find, in the record fixing the boundaries between Charlestown and Cambridge, the agreement that "all the lands impaled by Newe Towne men, with the necke thereunto adjoyneing whereon Mr. Graves dwelleth, shall belong to said New Towne." Mayhap it was this same Thomas Graves who laid out the town of Woburn in 1640, but at any rate he sold his house in October, 1635, to Mr. Atherton Haugh, and in August, 1706, it was transferred to Spencer Phips, and belonged to Lt.-Gov. Phips when he died in his mansion, the Winthrop Place, on Arrow Street, near Bow, in 1757.

But the major part of the Cambridge houses were grouped south of Harvard Square to the river, the first — which burned in 1666 — being started by Thomas Dudley, on what is now Dunster Street, early in 1631.

The dwelling of Thomas Hooker, as well as of his succeeding ministers, stood where Boylston Hall now is — and the house of the first president of Harvard, Henry Dunster, as well as the place where Stephen Daye's printing press was first set up, stood about where Massachusetts Hall stands.

Away from Tory Row and its environs, the old Hicks House is now located at the corner of Boylston and South streets. It was built in 1760 at the corner of Dunster and Winthrop streets by John Hicks, a master carpenter, for his own home. He was born in 1725, and participated in the Boston Tea Party, but was killed while fighting the retreating British from Lexington, on April 19, 1775. After his death, the building was used by General Putnam as an office.

In 1929, its destruction was threatened by a Harvard building plan, but through the efforts of the Cambridge Historical Society it was saved and moved to the present location where it is now used as a library for one of the new Harvard college houses.

Previous to 1850, the John Vassall House was the only

one on that side of Brattle Street for almost three-quarters of a mile, from Ash Street to Elmwood. A part of the western end of this house was probably built in 1636, by William Adams, on a site that was then outside the palisade. In 1682 it came into the possession of Capt. Andrew Belcher, whose son inherited the house in 1717 and married the daughter of Lt.-Gov. Partridge of New Hampshire. He later

ope Royall, of Medford, and enlarged the house for her upon its eastern side five years later in 1746.

The Marble Chamber, in this newer portion, was so called in a sworn inventory of Henry Vassall's estate, dated 8 September 1769.

His widow, Mrs. Vassall, removed to Antigua, leaving her "medicine chest," at the request of the Provincial Congress. Only one other such chest, at

Hall and Staircase in Portion Added by Maj. Henry Vassall in 1746
JOHN VASSALL HOUSE—1686—94 BRATTLE STREET, CAMBRIDGE, MASSACHUSETTS

served twenty-seven years as Royal Governor of Massachusetts, New Hampshire, and New Jersey. John Vassall came into possession in 1736. He had married Elizabeth, daughter of Lt.-Gov. Spencer Phips, in 1734. His son, Maj. John, Jr., who built the Vassall-Craigie-Longfellow House in 1759, was born here, as well as a daughter, Elizabeth, who married Thomas Oliver, who built "Elmwood."

Col. Henry Vassall, a brother of John, Sr., took over the property in 1741, and shortly after married Penel-

Roxbury, was then available to the newly formed American army, and Vassall House became the medical headquarters under Dr. Church, who with Dr. Foster, lived and ran the army hospital there.

The plan is unusual, with two separate halls and staircases, to west and east, the space between—originally open, with a bay toward the river—having been comparatively recently filled in by a central room, with a beam supported by Doric columns. In 1841 a fire damaged the eastern part of the house, burning the roof and five dormers then on that side.

Thomas Oliver built "Elmwood" shortly after his marriage to Elizabeth Vassall, granddaughter of Lt.-Gov. Phips, in 1760, and just after the land had been transferred from Watertown to Cambridge, in 1754. His maternal grandmother, Mrs. James Brown of Antigua, married Isaac Royall of Medford as her second husband. Oliver became Lieutenant Governor in

the first floor (the fireplace was shown in the previous chapter) until 1876, when he moved into the room in front of it, on the southeast corner of the house, shown on page 143.

"The Larches" was built in 1808, and with its furnishings is one of the most beautiful of the Cambridge houses. The present owners are Mr. & Mrs. Henry D. Tudor, Mrs. Tudor being the great-granddaughter of

The Marble Chamber, 1746
JOHN VASSALL HOUSE—1686—94 BRATTLE STREET, CAMBRIDGE, MASSACHUSETTS

1774, just in time to be mobbed by the populace on September 2 of that year. The house was used as a hospital during the British occupation of Boston. "Elmwood" was later occupied by Elbridge Gerry of Marblehead, a signer of the Declaration of Independence, Governor of Massachusetts and Vice-President of the U.S. In 1818 it came into possession of Rev. Charles Lowell, pastor of the West Church, Boston (1806–1845), the father of James Russell Lowell.

The latter used as his study the southwest room on

William Gray, who built the house, and was Lieutenant Governor of the Commonwealth of Massachusetts in 1811—at which time Elbridge Gerry was Governor and lived at "Elmwood," nearby.

The general style of the architecture is markedly similar to the houses of the noted Salem architect, Samuel McIntire, especially in the delicacy of the over-doors and mantel pieces, for which McIntire was justly famous. The stair hall wall paper is over one hundred years old, and the long parlor at the left, with

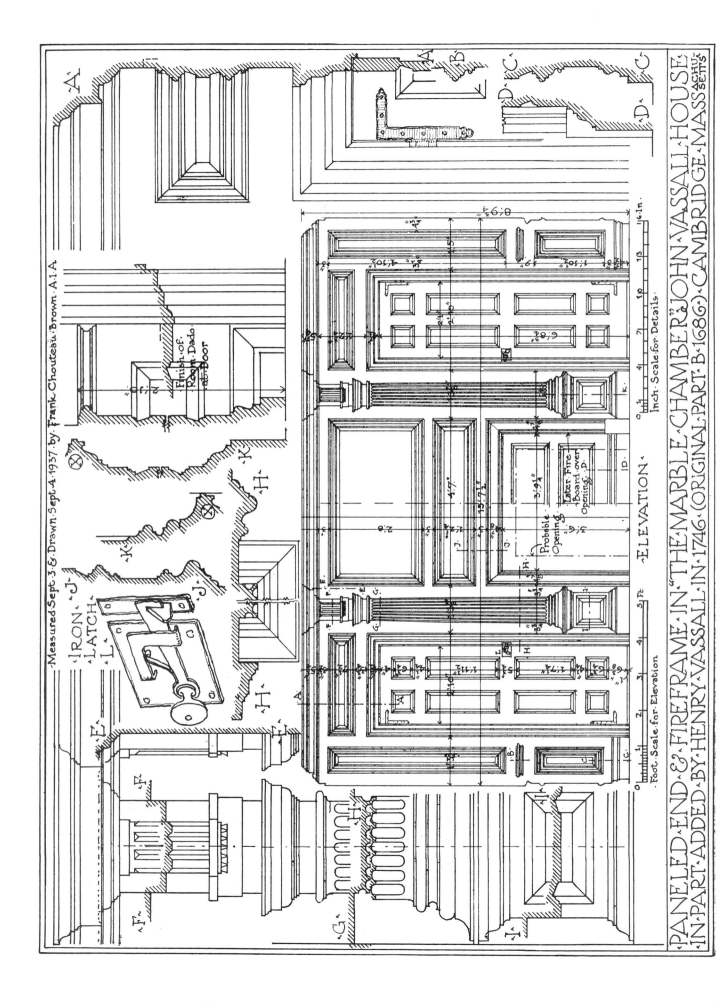

Measured Sept. 3. & Drawn Sept. 4. 1937. by. Frank. Chouteau. Brown. A.1.A.

·A·
·A·
·B·
·C·
·D·
·D·
·C·

Finish. of. Room. Dado. at. Door

·IRON· ·J· ·LATCH· ·L·

·K·
·H·
·J·
·K·
·E·
·H·
·A·
·B·
·C·
·F·
·G·
·I·

8·9¾"
16·In

Inch. Scale for. Details.

Probable Opening.
Later. Fire board. over Opening. D.

·ELEVATION·

Foot. Scale. for. Elevation

·PANELED·END·&·FIREFRAME·IN·"THE·MARBLE·CHAMBER·JOHN·VASSALL·HOUSE
·IN·PART·ADDED·BY·HENRY·VASSALL·IN·1746·(ORIGINAL·PART·B·1686)·CAMBRIDGE·MASSACHUSETTS

Front Hall and Staircase Detail
"ELMWOOD"—1760—CORNER OF
MT. AUBURN STREET AND ELMWOOD AVENUE

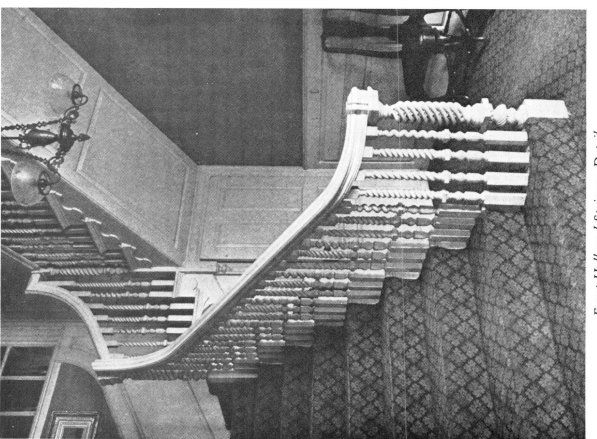

Front Hall and Staircase Detail
VASSALL-CRAIGIE-LONGFELLOW HOUSE—1759—
CAMBRIDGE, MASSACHUSETTS

Mantel and End, Southwest Room, First Floor

VASSALL-CRAIGIE-LONGFELLOW HOUSE—1759—105 BRATTLE STREET, CAMBRIDGE, MASSACHUSETTS

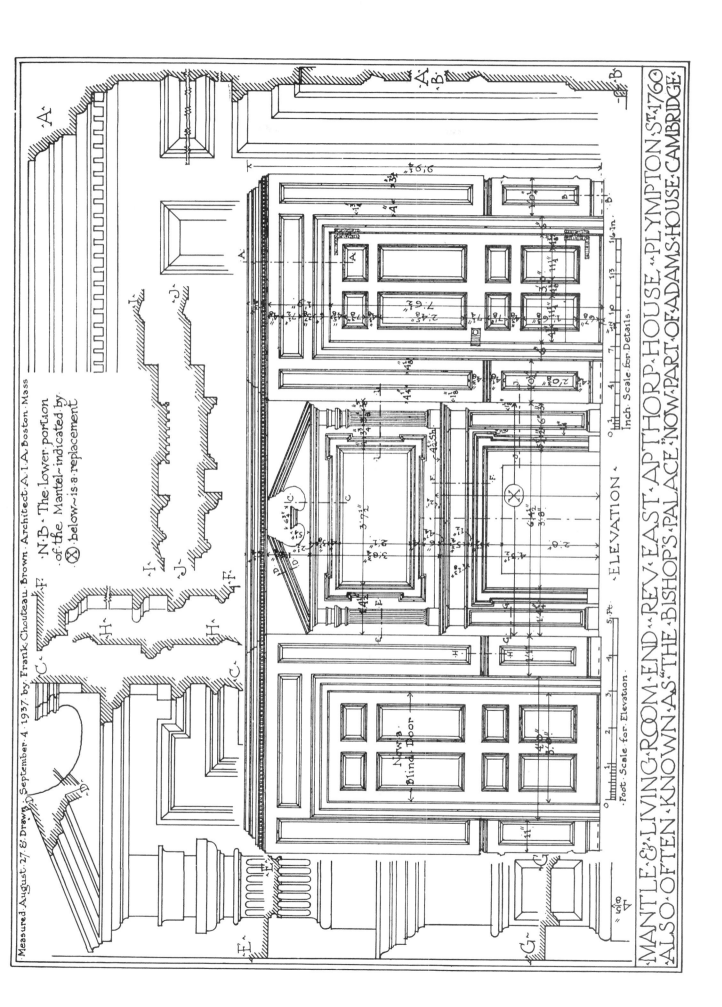

Measured August 27 & Drawn September 4 1937 by Frank Chouteau Brown Architect A.I.A. Boston Mass

N.B. The lower portion of the Mantel indicated by ⊗ below is a replacement

Now a Blind Door

ELEVATION

Foot Scale for Elevation.
Inch Scale for Details.

MANTLE & LIVING ROOM END REV. EAST APTHORP HOUSE "PLYMPTON ST. 1760 ALSO OFTEN KNOWN AS "THE BISHOP'S PALACE" NOW PART OF ADAMS HOUSE CAMBRIDGE

Detail of Mantel in Living Room
APTHORP HOUSE — 1761 — 15 PLYMPTON STREET, CAMBRIDGE, MASSACHUSETTS

Mantel and Paneled End, Northeast Room, Second Floor

Mantel and End, Southeast Room, First Floor

"ELMWOOD"—1760—CORNER MT. AUBURN STREET AND ELMWOOD AVENUE
CAMBRIDGE, MASSACHUSETTS

its eight windows and two fireplaces, still maintains the atmosphere of the early years of the nineteenth century.

CHRIST CHURCH

Four meeting houses were in use in Cambridge before the present Christ Church was erected. The fourth edifice was raised, November 17, 1756, and the

eign Parts, to have a Church of England established in Cambridge, and the Rev. East Apthorp was appointed Missionary to Cambridge by that Society, in 1759. He had been born in Boston and had just graduated from Jesus College, Oxford, in Old England. Along with the first six petitioners named, he was made a member of the building committee.

The committee agreed that the dimensions, includ-

JOHN HICKS HOUSE — 1762 — BOYLSTON AND SOUTH STREETS, CAMBRIDGE, MASSACHUSETTS

first service was held, July 24, 1757. It continued in use until 1833; but in 1759 a subscription was held for another church edifice in the town, and on October 15, 1761, the new Christ Church, Episcopal, was opened. Previously, Henry Vassall, Joseph Lee, John Vassall, Ralph Inman, Thomas Oliver, David Phips, Robert Temple, and James Apthorp had petitioned the English Society for the Propagation of the Gospel in For-

ing walls, but not chancel and tower, be sixty feet long by forty-five feet wide; that "the architect be at liberty to make any alteration in these dimensions, provided he does not enlarge the area"; that the building be of wood, with one tier of windows, and no gallery except an organ loft; that the cost not exceed £500 sterling; that Mr. Harrison, of Newport, be requested for "a plan and elevation of the outside and inside,

Detail of Staircase and Hallway
"THE LARCHES"—1808—22 LARCH ROAD, CAMBRIDGE, MASSACHUSETTS

Details of Three Doorhead Treatments
"THE LARCHES" — 1808 — 22 LARCH ROAD, CAMBRIDGE, MASSACHUSETTS

and of the pulpit and vestry of the church, and if Mr. Harrison approves of it, there be no steeple, only a tower with a belfry; and that he be informed of the dimensions of a picture designed for the chancel." The dimensions of the building were adopted by the architect, Mr. Peter Harrison, who had also designed King's Chapel in Boston and the Redwood Library in Newport, but the cost ran to about £1300. The exterior, originally requested "to be of rough cast,"

monial they had always associated with religion overseas and had come to this country to escape. Popular feeling ran high, and this opposition—headed by Dr. Mayhew, of the West Church in Boston—finally made the Rev. Apthorp's position so trying that he returned to England in 1764.

During the Revolution the building suffered badly. Its Tory congregation were all forced to leave with the British, and the church was closed—although there is

Entrance Front
"THE LARCHES"—1808—22 LARCH ROAD, CAMBRIDGE, MASSACHUSETTS

was never applied. The church appears today much as it did then, except for the introduction of two bays, which added twenty-three feet to its length; but on the inside the hour-glass pulpit and box pews are gone.

Most of the church proprietors lived on Brattle Street; also known as Tory Row or Church Lane, and had earlier belonged to King's Chapel in Boston. Disfavor was aroused by the beautiful and pretentious "palace," built by the young rector for himself and wife near the college grounds. Both represented—to the other residents of the town—the power and cere-

a record that, on the last Sunday in 1775, the service was read at the request of Mrs. Washington, who had arrived December 11th; but Capt. Chester's company from Wethersfield, Connecticut, was quartered in the building, and melted window lights and organ pipes for bullets. After the army left, the church was again closed, but on June 19, 1778, a young officer of Burgoyne's Army who had died, was interred in the Vassall tomb beneath the church, and Americans plundered the building, destroyed the pulpit, reading desk, and communion table, and broke the bellows and pipes.

General View from East, Across Old Burial Ground
CHRIST CHURCH—1761—GARDEN STREET, CAMBRIDGE, MASSACHUSETTS

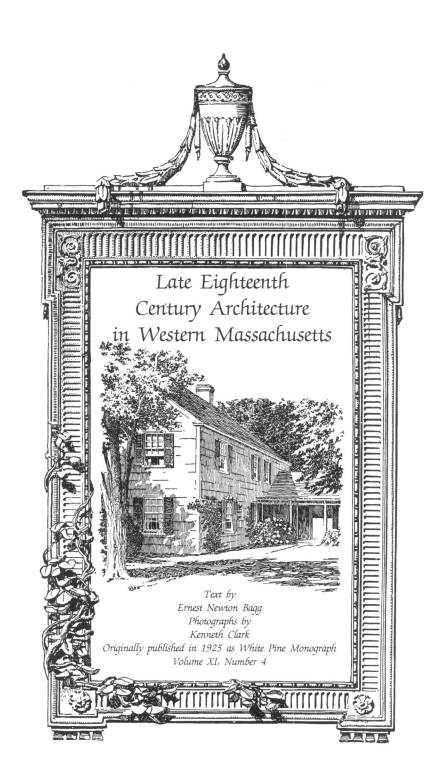

Late Eighteenth
Century Architecture
in Western Massachusetts

Text by
Ernest Newton Bagg
Photographs by
Kenneth Clark
Originally published in 1925 as White Pine Monograph
Volume XI, Number 4

BOICE (RICE) HOUSE, SOUTH PLEASANT STREET, AMHERST, MASSACHUSETTS
Built by Horace Kellogg about 1828

LATE EIGHTEENTH CENTURY ARCHITECTURE IN WESTERN MASSACHUSETTS

THE Pilgrim Fathers, by reputation straight-laced and quite given to denying themselves and families many things which would not be termed extravagances by moderns, had many redeeming qualities, among them a shrewd and calculating intelligence and unquenchable ambition.

The Connecticut Valley settlers, once in possession of their rugged and somewhat threatening promised land, were for only a short time content with their primitive shelters and hastily thrown-together barricades. Some of their earliest buildings suggest the severe outlines of such structures as the gloomy gaol in that old Chelmsford-Springfield whence came many settlers of this region. That is, from the town, not the gaol!

The proper cultivation of newly-cleared land, and study of the elements necessary to make it produce food in the shortest possible space of time interested these pioneers far more at that time than what style of house would best suit each man's particular corner of the lovely New England landscape. Their sterling womenfolk were undoubtedly prime and potent factors in the inevitable reaction. Windows here, conveniences for housekeeping there, enlargements of space in first one direction, then another, and most of them suggested by necessity. These changes increased with the lessening of danger from terrors by night and arrows by day. The tendency toward lines of beauty in building at first showed itself as a matter of course, with the wealthier immigrants, whom their neighbors were not slow to imitate. Ornament as well as utility was added as each settler prospered and felt that he could afford to do so. The decades swiftly passed and it can not be denied that now-existing examples of western New England homebuilding possess many features of artistic as well as purely architectural charm.

Among leaf-embowered homesteads on each side of Longmeadow's principal street—a veritable "royal greensward, fit for camp of kings"—one of the glimpses longest remembered by tourists with an eye for sheer beauty of setting, is the Alexander Field House.

Anciently the Indian "Massacksic," this was "land to be desired" indeed! It was this same broad, ample stretch of "ye longe meddowe" lying next south of the 1636 Springfield plantation, which attracted the shrewd settlers. It should be recorded that they very early showed signs of appreciation of beautiful home-site surroundings, and were ill-content with lands mainly suitable for farming.

Quaint old records show how, in 1703, Daniel, Benjamin and Lieut. Joseph Cooley and a dozen neighbors in the lowlands next the "Great River" petitioned the parent town for leave to possess home-lots on "Convenient and better land out of the general field, on the hil," because floods have "put o^r Lives in g^{rt} Danger, o^r housing much damnifyed, & many cattle are Lost." The Alexander Field House stands upon the original six-lot grant assigned to the Cooleys. This grant extended for 120 rods along the ancient "commons" highway, laid out 330 feet wide—and almost as far back towards the river. The Field family arrived in Longmeadow about 1728, and through marriages with the Cooleys came into possession of the site near the head of magnificent Longmeadow Street.

Scarcely a mile in a bee line (thrice that around by nearest bridge way) lies the eldest settlement of western Massachusetts, Agawam; first choice of the pioneers as a site for Springfield. The first dwelling in this region erected by white man was the rough shelter placed in the famous "House meadow" at the north end of Agawam, by William Pynchon's henchmen, Cable and Woodcock, in the summer of 1635. It was abandoned within the year because of the danger from floods; and the Springfield River bank was for the next two centuries the heart of "town," since 'twas ever best to be on the safer side. It is architecturally interesting to note in passing that the next year's record states that this house was "built at the common charge for six pounds!"

In the heart of the old town, on the east side of the

wide, elm-arched street where, on the afternoon of June 30, 1775, General Washington passed, bound for Cambridge where the new Continental Army awaited its commander-in-chief, stands the fine old Leonard dwelling built in 1808. Both upstairs and down, the middle section of the house is all hallway, about twelve by forty feet, with handsome paneled doors leading into ample rooms on each side. Some of the big fireplace openings have the wide flagging hearthstones fitted into the flooring, the latter still containing many of the original broad boards. On the ground floor the doors, cut in half, allowed the serving of flip and cider over the lower closed part. "Side-fire" bake-ovens, hand-wrought door-latches, and nail-heads, and hand-hewn foundation timbers are interesting features of this one of the most substantial houses of its era in Agawam. A curious detail of the side door (page 165) is the hinged halving, from top to bottom rather than the frequent side-to-side treatment. Old residents aver that the latch-half of the door was opened mainly to answer inquiries; and that the full forty inches of opening was thrown wide when answers and inquiries proved satisfactory to all concerned.

West Springfield, which once included in its twelve-mile length both Agawam and Holyoke is now separated from the former by the Agawam River. In the eastern edge of its central part, on a lordly location overlooking miles of Connecticut River Valley, and directly across the river from Dr. J. G. Holland's famous Brightwood, stands the old First Congregational Church, the cornerstone of which is marked "June, 1800." The townspeople of that day had long been dissatisfied with the primitive "church-on-the-common," forty-two feet square and built a century before that. John Ashley, a prosperous parishioner, seeing the inhabitants could not agree upon a location for a more modern building, terminated a long and rather violent controversy on the question, by coming forward with an offer of thirteen hundred pounds on condition that the "spacious and elegant meeting house" of the photographs should be placed "on a spot designated by me": and thus the old "white church on the hill" came into being, where all the different factions of town could look up to it. It was built "on honor" as well as on a foundation of red sandstone; and its hand-hewn timbers of white oak are found to be sound and staunch to this day. The very young contractor, Captain Timothy Billings of Deerfield, aged twenty-eight! received about $1400—part of it in St. Croix rum—for building it. Ashley and Billings, consulting with the famous Dr. Lathrop, who was then minister of the church, were responsible for its architecture, which has

been greatly admired. In style it is a rather less severely simple modification of the Christopher Wren pattern, examples of which are quite numerous in New England.

Another condition made by the donor of the money for this church was that the building should be used as a church for a hundred years. After a full century, plus a dozen years more for good measure, it was sold to become a Masonic temple; and another church building was adopted close to the historic spot where the ancient building of controversy had been established. Sacred relics of the beautiful old church on the hill, such as carved ornaments from the sides of its high square pulpit, and paneled pew doors, have been built into some of the houses of the neighborhood, as a reminder of the "Mt. Orthodox" that used to be!

Old Hadley, and that newer part long known as East Hadley—which is now Amherst—have some charming old dwellings, with the hip and gambrel roof as well as fanlight suggestions of the good taste and imagination of the elders in architecture. The houses were first of all built to withstand the rigors of the once savage New England winters, and moreover were built to last. They blossom out, unexpectedly, into fanciful bits of ornamentation here and there, some perhaps accidental, but many more by design.

The old Boice place, on South Pleasant Street, Amherst, now owned and occupied by the Rice family, is one of the particularly noteworthy specimens of late eighteenth century homebuilding. It was built about 1828 by the farmer-carpenter, Horace Kellogg. That he was a man of uncommonly good judgment becomes apparent when it is known that he was on the building committee having in charge the erection of the much-admired third building of the First Congregational Church; the same which was transformed into what is now the stately College Hall. Other specimens of the Kellogg taste in such matters are found elsewhere in the eastern part of Hampshire County in buildings which not only wear but look well with which he had to do either as a builder or in an advisory capacity. The family of Sanford Boice, by which the place is now generally known, occupied it for the first twenty years of the present century.

The Hubbard House (page 166) in Northampton, so called from one of its earlier owners, was built in 1744 by a grandson of Cornet Joseph Parsons to whom the original grant of land was made and who was slain by the Indians of King Philip in 1675. As a precaution against Indian attack by day (the last recorded tragedy from this source was the killing of Elisha Clark of Northampton, August 1747) strong wooden shutters were placed in front of each first floor window.

FIRST CONGREGATIONAL CHURCH, WEST SPRINGFIELD, MASSACHUSETTS
Built in 1800 to replace first "Church-on-the-Common" built in 1702

Detail of Spire
FIRST CONGREGATIONAL CHURCH, WEST SPRINGFIELD
The bell in the tower was recast from the one used in the 1702 church

CHARLES LEONARD HOUSE, AGAWAM CENTER, MASSACHUSETTS
Built in 1808 on the Agawam Commons

CHARLES LEONARD HOUSE, AGAWAM CENTER, MASSACHUSETTS

Built in 1808 by Chas. Leonard, a farmer-graduate of Harvard, at one end of his great farm

FIELD HOUSE, LONGMEADOW, MASSACHUSETTS

Detail of Central Portion of Main Façade
FIELD HOUSE, LONGMEADOW, MASSACHUSETTS

Detail of Column and Entablature, Front Doorway
FIELD HOUSE, LONGMEADOW, MASSACHUSETTS

FRONT · ELEVATION
scale 1/8" = 1'·0"

Brick

Roof originally of shingles.

House now has cement terrace at front & side - this is a much later addition.

Wing at rear is late addition

Stone

SID

1/4 FULL SIZE OF MAIN CORNICE

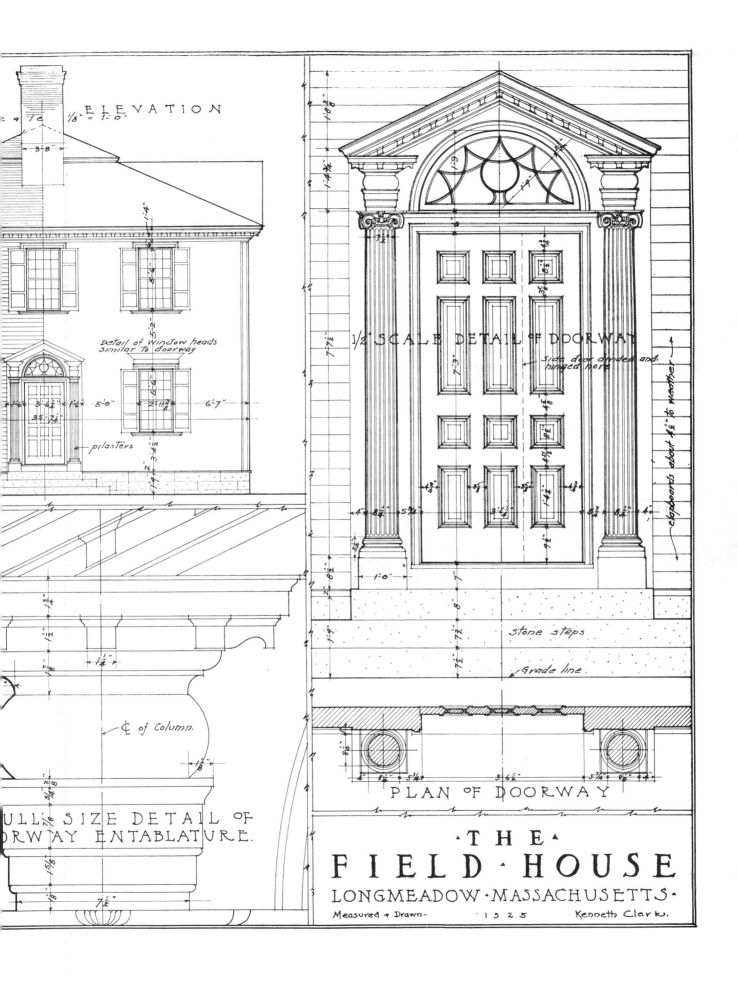

ELEVATION ⅛" = 1'-0"

3'-8"

5'-4"

5'-2"

detail of window heads
similar to doorway

5'-6"

pilasters

5'-0"   2'-11⅜"   6'-7"

35'-7¼"

1'-6" 3'-4¼" 1'-4"

7'-7" 2" 3'-4½"

¾"

1½"

⅞"   1¼"
⅛"

ℭ of Column.

1⅛"

3⅜"
⅝"   ¾"
7⁄8"

1⅝"

⅞"

7½"

FULL SIZE DETAIL OF
DOORWAY ENTABLATURE.

1'-0⅝"

1'-4¾"

7'-7½"

½" SCALE DETAIL OF DOORWAY

1'-9"

1'-9"

½"

Side door divided and
hinged here

7'-3"

clapboards about 4½" to weather

6½"   4½"

3⅜"   4⅛"

4½"   4½"
8¼"

1¼"   6½"
4"

4¼"   1'-4"   4¾"
3½"

4¼"   8¾"   5¼"
3'-6½"

8¼"   8¼"   4"

⅛"   8"   5¼"
2"   8½"
1½"   7"

1'-0"

1'-9"   7½"   8"
7½"   7½"

stone steps

Grade line.

8"
6¾"

4"   8¼"   5¼"
3'-6½"
5¾"   8¼"   4"

PLAN OF DOORWAY

·THE·
FIELD·HOUSE
LONGMEADOW·MASSACHUSETTS·
Measured + Drawn—   1925   Kenneth Clark.

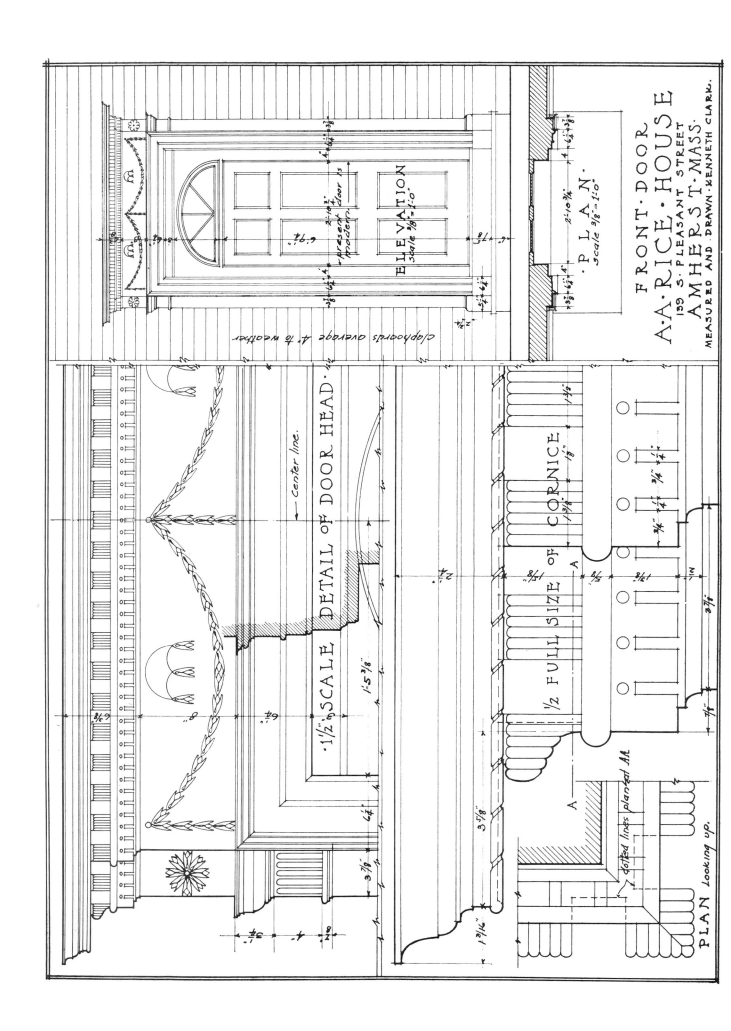

ELEVATION
Scale ⅛" = 1'-0"

present door is modern.

clapboards average 4" to weather.

PLAN
Scale ⅜" = 1'-0"

FRONT DOOR
A·A·RICE·HOUSE
159 S. PLEASANT STREET
AMHERST·MASS.
MEASURED AND DRAWN·KENNETH CLARK.

· 1½" SCALE · DETAIL OF DOOR HEAD ·

Center line.

½ FULL SIZE OF CORNICE

A   A

dotted lines plaster at AA

PLAN Looking up.

Detail of Front Doorway
BOICE (RICE) HOUSE, AMHERST, MASSACHUSETTS

Front Elevation

BOICE (RICE) HOUSE, AMHERST, MASSACHUSETTS

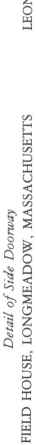

Detail of Side Doorway
LEONARD HOUSE, AGAWAM CENTER, MASSACHUSETTS

Detail of Side Doorway
FIELD HOUSE, LONGMEADOW, MASSACHUSETTS

Detail of South Window, Built in 1744 by Josiah Parsons

HUBBARD HOUSE, NORTHAMPTON, MASSACHUSETTS

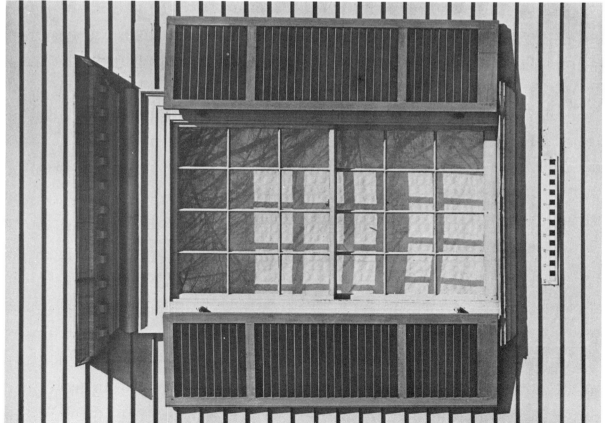

Detail of Window

FIELD HOUSE, LONGMEADOW, MASSACHUSETTS

Side Elevation
FIELD HOUSE, LONGMEADOW, MASSACHUSETTS

Central Motive
FIELD HOUSE, LONGMEADOW, MASSACHUSETTS

Dwellings of
Newbury Old Town

Text by
Frank Chouteau Brown
Photographs by
Arthur C. Haskell
Originally published in 1933 as White Pine Monograph
Volume XIX, Number 2

Entrance Detail
SPENCER-PIERCE-LITTLE HOUSE—1650—NEWBURY, MASSACHUSETTS

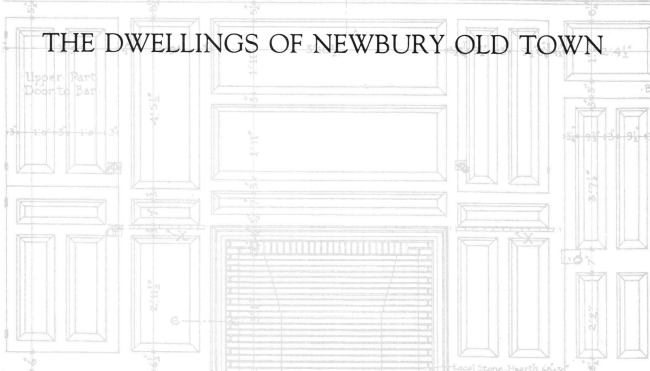

THE DWELLINGS OF NEWBURY OLD TOWN

CONTINUING further to trace the gradual development of our early domestic architecture in the eastern settlements during the seventeenth century, we may turn to the older section of Newbury, Massachusetts, to provide some pertinent and definite illustrations. The early small two-room story-and-a-half cottage, with chimney at one end, was soon supplanted by the full two-story house with end chimney —as in the original portions of the Coffin and Swett dwellings at "Ould Newbury," dating from about 1653 and 1670, respectively.

Both types were soon enlarged, by adding other rooms beyond the chimneys; or in some of the ways particularly described herewith—or they were supplanted by the larger plan, with central chimney and staircase against its southern face, with living "hall" at one side, and the principal family sleeping chamber at the other. This obvious and simple arrangement was soon supplemented by the separate kitchen at the back of the chimney—usually in a lean-to at the rear.

Next, one or both of the end spaces might be divided into two rooms—the rear ones upon the second floor being reached by another stairway in the lean-to; and then the plans' final amplification might be made by substituting end chimneys for the large central one, thus allowing the central hallway to extend through the house to reach the rear as well as the front rooms, upon both upper and lower floors.

Among these Newbury Old Town dwellings, the Jackman-Willett House itself illustrates the next step beyond the original Riggs House at Riverdale, Cape Ann (Volume III, Chapter 14), in the story-and-a-half cottage—now with three rooms upon the ground floor; while the Tristram Coffin House shows—although with a difference, itself almost unique!—the favorite method of adding a new and fully developed plan upon one end of the earlier southern-fronted cottage, leaving it to function as a kitchen ell, and establishing a new frontage to either east or west, toward a main highway. And, finally, the Swett-Ilsley grouping shows a more extensive arrangement of an early house extension, as in the Riggs dwelling, but here that process has been extended over a period of fully a hundred and fifty years, while at the same time changing the direction of growth—all as will more fully appear in detail in the accompanying text.

It was in 1634 that the Rev. Thomas Parker, of Newbury in Old England, arrived in New England with Nicholas Noyes, John Spencer and nearly an hundred other followers, on the *Mary and John*. They made their "landing" on the shores of the Quascacunquen, now the Parker, River; very near where the Old Bay Road from Ipswich to Newburyport now crosses that stream—and the earliest settlement was upon the northern bank, although in 1642 most of the settlers removed to more fertile land a few miles further northward, where each freeholder was given a "house lot of 4 akers," in the area still known as Newbury Old Town. And here the original Noyes Home still stands, near the Lower Green, although it has been so added to and changed — both within and without — that little remains to substantiate its early date (of about 1645 or 1646) except its huge timbers and summers, themselves largely out of sight above the lowered plaster ceilings added in later years.

Along with the Spencer-Pierce House, now usually known as the Little House, nearby — but of an ancient character still apparent despite the changes and additions that were made some hundred or more years ago — it is probably the most ancient among the early dwellings of this old part of Newbury. But the latter's cross-shaped plan; its thick stone walls, and old kitchen chimney (at the end of what is the northern arm of the cross — the southern portion being the unusual brick gable or "porch") make it unique among Massachusetts early house architecture — its nearest counterpart being probably the Old Stone House (1640) at Guilford, Connecticut. It, too, was probably built very near 1645 by either the original holder, John Spencer — or it may have been a few years later, by one Daniel Pierce, who bought the land of John Spencer's son in 1651.

Not only was the Coffin family prolific in the number of its human descendants, but also in its architectural products, as well. Tristram, the first of that name in the new world, was an old Royalist, who arrived in Haverhill, Massachusetts, from Brixton, Devonshire, in 1642, and first settled at Salisbury, near the mouth of the Merrimac. In December, 1647, he was granted the ferry privilege at "Newbury side," as well as keeping an "ordinary," or inn. But by 1653 the original part of the present Tristram Coffin structure, a two-story building with one room on the first floor and two on the second, with a chimney at its eastern end — now a part of the rearmost section of the house — was certainly in existence; as on March 2 of that year his son, Tristram, Jr., married Mrs. Somersby (née Judith Greenleaf) a widow, and was living there. It is even possible that this may have been a still earlier structure — belonging to the widow herself!

Meanwhile, his father, Tristram Coffin, Sr., removed to Nantucket in 1659 or 1660; and there the name of the family has been perpetuated on what is now the oldest house on the island, the Jethro Coffin House, built about 1686.

The original house had faced south, as was usual, with its doorway in front of the chimney near its eastern corner. Tristram, Jr., died February 4, 1704, aged 72 years, and in his will left his "dwelling hous" to his son Nathaniel. About 1693 the frame of another building was moved up to within thirteen or fourteen feet of the easterly end of the older house, and

what is the southeastern portion of the new front part of the dwelling was finished off, the old chimney rebuilt — or torn down and built anew — along with the intermediate portion necessary to connect the two sections. It is the fireplace in this chimney, and this room, that is shown in the measured drawing and accompanying photographs, though some of the finish may be of a still later date.

There seems to be some doubt whether the entire eastern front plan, as it appears now, was built at this time; or whether the central hallway and door in the middle of the street front, along with the rooms at the right or northern end of this new frontage were added at the time of the marriage of Nathaniel's son, Joseph, on July 15, 1725. In that event, the finish of the room shown here might have been renewed either then, or possibly shortly after Nathaniel's death, when 80 years old, on February 20, 1749.

Finally, either in 1725 — or at some subsequent period before 1785 — there was added a room at the back or northerly side of the original house to make a kitchen for the new front northerly portion; just as the rooms at the east and west of the oldest chimney were also in use as kitchens to serve the — at least! — three Coffin families that were simultaneously living in the old homestead!

The girt shown a few feet in front of the fireplace, shown in the drawing on page 175, is paralleled by another exposed a few feet beyond the western side of the same chimney, showing the portions that were added to these two rooms when the chimney was rebuilt and the two sections connected; while a slight bend in the southern length of the present building suggests to the careful observer that something a little out of the usual had probably here taken place. It is this intermediate section that is unusual — almost unique — in the records of enlarging early colonial dwellings! While another unique feature is to be found in the old buttery contained within the front portion of the dwelling, which has remained undisturbed from its original upfitting for almost two hundred years.

The other most interesting local dwelling is the Swett-Ilsley House — now again a hostelry! — which represents the changing backgrounds of over a hundred and fifty years in its various additions, without — as it fortunately happens — any of the later additions much obscuring or changing the work that had gone before. Along with the Tristram Coffin House, it is now owned by the Society for the Preservation of New England Antiquities, and therefore its preservation is assured — barring only the unfortunate accident of fire — for many years yet to come.

The building now faces east, fronting closely on the Old Bay Road, or High Street, only a few hundred feet beyond the more retired Coffin homestead. It has two front doorways, the one to the left admitting to the older portion. The two rooms on the first and second floors—at the left of and beyond this doorway—were the original house, then fronting south, with chimney at the west end and doorway and stairs to

against the eastern face of this chimney. The old west chimney was torn down; and a small corner fireplace built against the west side of the new chimney to heat the small room that occupied the space previously taken by chimney and staircase; and the ridgepole was changed to run from north to south instead of from

JACKMAN-WILLETT HOUSE—1696—NEWBURY OLD TOWN, MASSACHUSETTS

the south of it, in the southwest corner, with a slight front second-story overhang.

The ridgepole then ran from east to west; and this portion was built by Stephen Swett, at least as early as 1670. It may even have been several years older than that, as the chamfers on the timbers are very like those in the oldest part of the Coffin House. The frame shows where two and three mullion casement windows were set, one of these being about where the fireplace and chimney are now on the north side of the old hall.

The next and most important change was made previous to 1700, probably between 1690 and 1695, when what is now the middle room was built at the north of the older house, with a chimney between the old part and the addition. A new stairway was built

east to west, as it had originally. The rear (west) lean-to was built on, probably between 1756 and 1760, to provide a new kitchen back of the large hall, with its enormous fireplace, one of the largest of the period now known in Massachusetts. And it is this room, or rather its south side with its unusual large fireplace, that is shown in detail in the measured drawing on page 180.

This middle room with its enormous fireplace has in its rear or western end a door and sashed opening that formerly connected with the serving "bar," during that portion of the structure's existence when it was in use as the Blue Anchor Tavern; this room then being the tap room, and the room in the lean-to behind being the kitchen—in substantiation of which arrangement there still exists built into the front angle

TRISTRAM COFFIN HOUSE — 1651–1693–1725 — NEWBURY OLD TOWN, MASSACHUSETTS

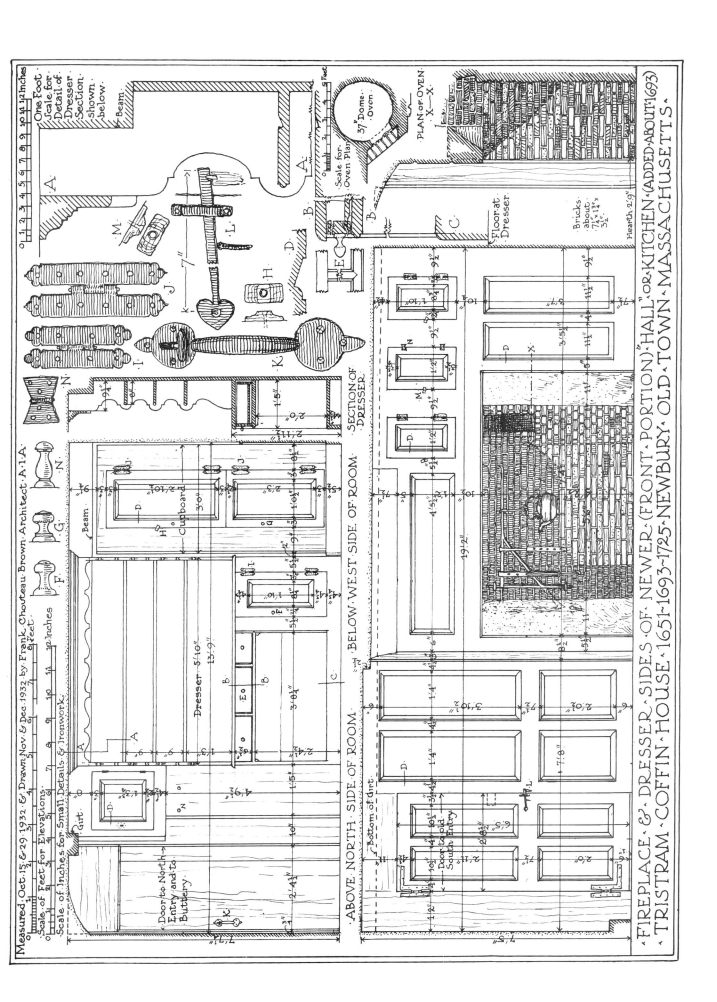

"FIREPLACE · & · DRESSER · SIDES · OF · NEWER · (FRONT · PORTION) · "HALL" · OR · KITCHEN · (ADDED · ABOUT · 1693)
· TRISTRAM · COFFIN · HOUSE · 1651~1693~1725 · NEWBURY · OLD · TOWN · MASSACHUSETTS ·

of this space, the remains of the old wall cupboard, of which the intermediate kitchen of the Coffin House still shows so good an example, the invariable adjunct of the seventeenth-century kitchen!

The house did not come into the possession of the Ilsley family until 1797. Meanwhile, during, and for a while previous to, the Revolution, it had served as an inn; seen the training of local companies of militia; watched the progress of the French and Indian Wars

tunately this was accomplished without any more disturbance than the closing of a few windows and the opening of a doorway into what then became the middle room, on both lower and upper floors.

While to the more curious, there is always in reserve the attic; that space that—in New England—has so often been kept inviolate, sacred to the housewives' desire for "order," to which proscribed precincts anything outmoded or otherwise cluttering up

Fireplace Side of Hall or Kitchen (Added About 1693)
TRISTRAM COFFIN HOUSE, NEWBURY OLD TOWN, MASSACHUSETTS

(the Merrimac River being really the northern frontier of the New England settlements at that time) and had at least one owner, John March, who was a captain in the attack on Canada in 1700, and later helped defend the Casco Bay fort against the French.

Still further to the north, the door, hallway, and room at its right, is the last addition that was made to the old dwelling—probably shortly after 1800. For-

the daily wheels of progress may always be exiled. There, amid dust and these ancient family treasures, the timber framing and changes in the house's history usually lie plainly outspread before any interested or trained observer.

Down nearer the original "landing," on the Parker River, are two old structures also worthy attention. One, the Richard Dole-Little House, illustrated on page 183, is the simple long lean-to dwelling, with its weathered ancient clapboarding, that still looks down toward the banks of the Parker River. Inside it has been much changed about to keep up with the progress and needs of its various families of occupants, but outside it certainly continues to look its years, from 1670, the date of its beginnings.

A little further north, at a sharp turn in the road, is the Samuel Seddon House; once another ordinary

taproom at the left, from near the rear line of the house, though if even this record is to be much longer preserved, steps must soon be taken to maintain the old frame and make the roof tight.

About midway from this old tavern to the center of Old Newbury, at the left side of the Old Post Road, is the location of the original Burying Ground, and beside it now is the Jackman-Willett House.

Richard Jackman was the youngest son of James

Dresser Side of Hall or Kitchen (Added About 1693)
TRISTRAM COFFIN HOUSE, NEWBURY OLD TOWN, MASSACHUSETTS

on the high road out of Boston. Built in 1728, its windows are now shuttered; its old central chimney has been taken out and replaced by two smaller ones, in order to gain the room for a central hallway upon the second floor; and its floors are gradually settling and sagging out of true. But, inside, it is still possible to trace the location of the "bar," opening into the

Jackman, the immigrant, who died in 1694, when Richard had been married thirteen years. When his father's estate was settled the following year, he built his new house, which was finished in 1696. He had married Elizabeth Plummer, and when her father— who had the ferry at the Parker River—died in 1702, Corporal Richard Jackman was appointed, on Septem-

Bedroom

Buttery

TRISTRAM COFFIN HOUSE, NEWBURY OLD TOWN, MASSACHUSETTS

SWETT-ILSLEY HOUSE — 1670–1700–1760 — NEWBURY OLD TOWN, MASSACHUSETTS

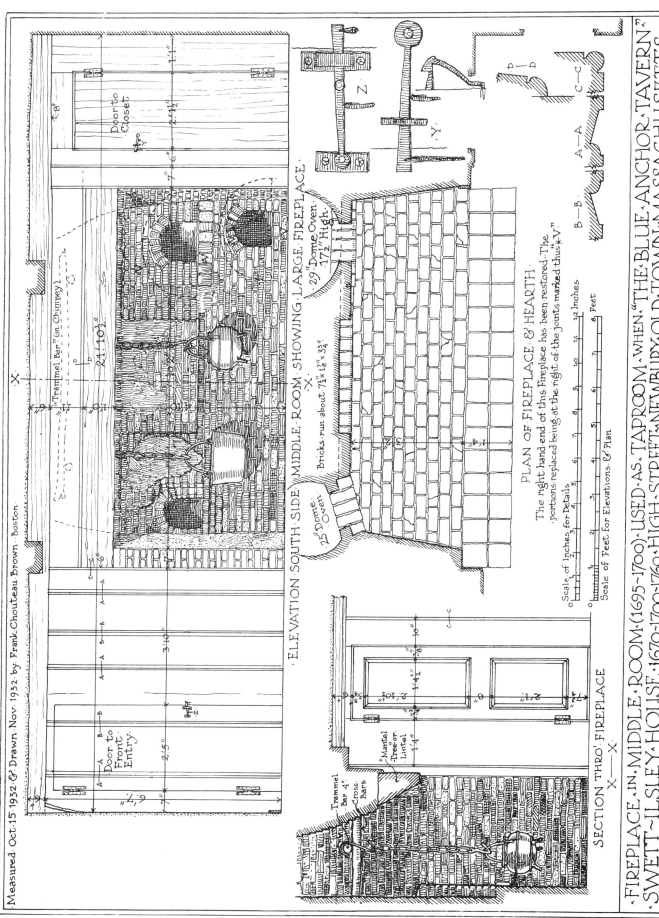

Measured Oct. 15. 1932. & Drawn. Nov. 1932. by. Frank. Chouteau. Brown. Boston.

Door to Closet

Door to Front Entry.

"Trammel Bar" on Chimney.

· ELEVATION · SOUTH · SIDE · MIDDLE · ROOM · SHOWING · LARGE · FIREPLACE ·
· X ·

Bricks. run. about. 7½ x 18 x 3¼.

25" Dome Oven.

29" Dome. Oven.
17½" High.

PLAN · OF · FIREPLACE · & · HEARTH ·

The. right. hand. end. of. this. Fireplace. has. been. restored.. The.
. portions. replaced. being. at. the. right. of. the. joints. marked. thus. "V".

Scale. of. Inches. for. Details

Scale. of. Feet. for. Elevations. & Plan

"Mantel Tree. or. Lintel

Trammel Bar &
Cross-Bars

SECTION · THRO' · FIREPLACE
X — X ·

·FIREPLACE· IN· MIDDLE· ROOM· (1695~1700)· USED· AS· TAPROOM· WHEN· "THE· BLUE· ANCHOR· TAVERN"·
·SWETT~ ILSLEY· HOUSE· 1670~1700~1760· HIGH· STREET~ NEWBURY· OLD· TOWN~ MASSACHUSETTS·

Fireplace in Middle Room (1695-1700)

SWETT-ILSLEY HOUSE — 1670-1700-1760 — HIGH STREET, NEWBURY OLD TOWN, MASSACHUSETTS

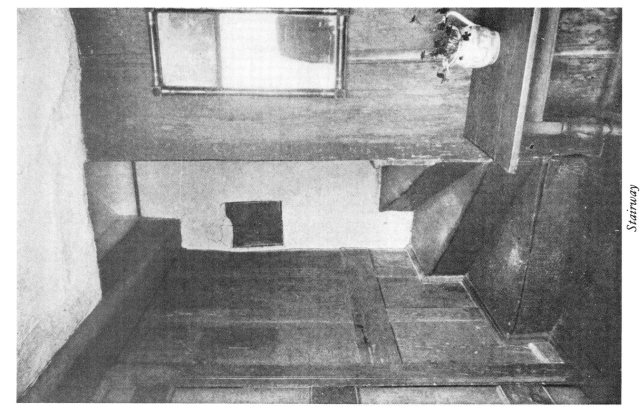

Stairway

Fireplace

SWETT-ILSLEY HOUSE — 1670–1700–1760 — NEWBURY OLD TOWN, MASSACHUSETTS

RICHARD DOLE-LITTLE HOUSE — 1670 — NEWBURY OLD TOWN, MASSACHUSETTS

ber 16, 1702, to "keep the ferry over Oldtown river, alias ye River Parker." At that time he was living in his new house, on a lot on the Ferry Road, across the street from the Seddon place.

By the summer of 1930 the little house had become so dilapidated that, when the "Sons and Daughters of the First Settlers of Newbury" undertook to put it into repair, as the oldest surviving primitive cottage then available, it was decided to move it a mile or so up

tage-houses of this locality is there to be obtained.

Again continuing north toward the Lower Green and the Port, the Dr. Peter Toppan House, of 1697, may be seen almost directly across the highway from the Swett-Ilsley place. It displays one of the most imposing gambrels of the locality, although the walls have been covered with new shingles, and the dwelling —for some time housing two families—has but recently been brought back to its single family ap-

NOYES HOUSE—c1645—NEWBURY OLD TOWN, MASSACHUSETTS

the Post road to a position beside the original Burying Ground, about midway between the Landing and the Lower Green. The cottage probably still shows its original outlines, though the work on the interior had not been completed at the time these pictures were taken. The old chimney had not then been rebuilt, but the quaint window trim and heads, the clapboarding and "jet" finish had been carried out along the old lines, so that a very good idea of the appearance of one of the simpler types of early cot-

pearance. Probably it could assume a well deserved place in a sequential record illustrating the development of the New England gambrel roof; but, located so closely adjacent to the Swett-Ilsley and Tristram Coffin houses, it cannot but be preferably grouped with them; leaving only the better known and distinctively different architecture of the Short House waiting for some later—and fuller—presentation; which, perhaps along with the Spencer-Pierce-Little House, its beauty and individuality entitle it to receive.

DR. PETER TOPPAN HOUSE — 1697 — NEWBURY OLD TOWN, MASSACHUSETTS

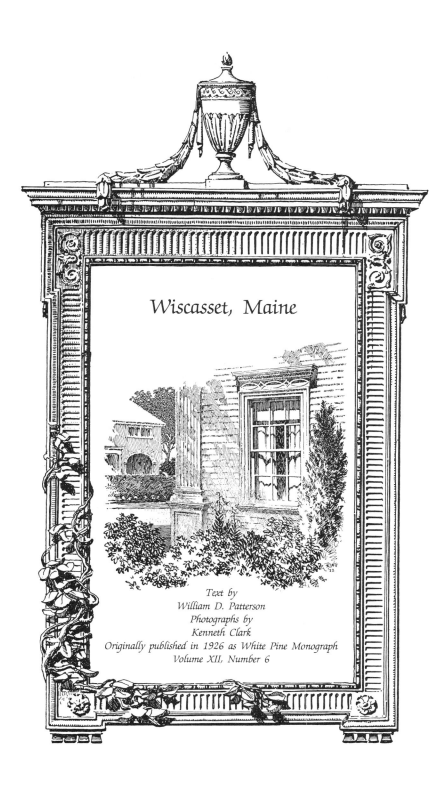

Wiscasset, Maine

Text by
William D. Patterson
Photographs by
Kenneth Clark
Originally published in 1926 as White Pine Monograph
Volume XII, Number 6

NICKELS-SORTWELL HOUSE, WISCASSET, MAINE

WISCASSET, MAINE

IT is claimed that DeMonts and Champlain, French pioneers in the New World, in the course of their exploration of the Maine coast, in 1605, ascended the Sheepscot River to what is now Wiscasset, and, although impressed with the beauty and majesty of its shores and the ease of access from the sea, they, learning that George Waymouth, the Englishman, had but a few weeks earlier planted the cross of St. George at what is now known as St. George's River as a token of discovery and possession, returned not hither. At what date Englishmen came to live here is not known with certainty; but it does appear from a deed given by three Indian sagamores of this river, in 1663, to George Davie, an English seaman, who is believed to have come hence from Cornwall or Devon, in England, that Davie was then a resident of the Sheepscot region. Here he continued until he and his family were driven away by Indians in the time of King Philip's War. He returned but was finally driven off with all the other white settlers here in the next Indian War. Under the deed mentioned, and subsequent deeds from the sagamores named, and by his rights by improvement and possession Davie claimed lands situate on both sides of the river and including the site of Wiscasset. Such rights descended to his heirs, from whom they passed by sale to persons interested in resettling the lands here, but the hardships of a frontier life retarded the growth of population following the beginning of such resettlement in 1729, and corporate existence was not attained until 1760.

Gradually a considerable export trade developed, consisting principally of forest products, such as white pine, oak and other primeval growths—a trade which was pursued with varying fortunes throughout the hardships of the Revolutionary War and the later spoliations by the French. The nineteenth century brought a remarkably prosperous expansion, the neutral position of our government with relation to the Napoleonic wars permitting cargoes to be carried into European ports under the United States flag, and it was facetiously said that Wiscasset milked the British cow. Although that period of roaring trade was short-lived, the wealth of the merchants and shipowners increased so greatly that it was soon reflected in all trades and professions and was signalized by the erection of the many fine mansions which are the distinguishing reminders of the briefly enduring fortunes of that time.

Conspicuous among such mansions is that which was built for Capt. William Nickels, a retired master mariner who had become largely interested in commerce and navigation, with resulting prosperity. Upon its site originally stood the first two-story house erected at Wiscasset Point. With increase of wealth, desiring greater luxury of living and expansion of his hospitality, he rolled the old house back to a lot but a few rods distant, where it now stands, and in 1807 and 1808 he caused a new house to be built. This house, with its lofty front and rich ornamentation of carving, has ever been an object of admiration, and passing tourists today stay their speed at sight of it. Tradition has it that two years' time was devoted to finishing its front hall; that the services of one man were required to keep its hearth fires of wood supplied through the winter seasons; that it was noted for its magnificent banquets and entertainments; and an inventory of its furnishings of that period reveals that this house was the abode of the cultured and wealthy. The more ancient Nickels manors, situate in Lincoln County, are still notable for their substantial and elaborate construction, but the mansion of William Nickels surpasses them all.

No less conspicuous in the time to which this writing relates were the houses of the Woods, headed by that of Gen. Abiel Wood, who began a long business life in Wiscasset as early as 1768 and whose title was derived from his connection with the Massachusetts militia. His three-story mansion, now demolished, stood near the shore and, although of earlier date than that of Captain Nickels, is said to have resembled it in size and wealth of detail. The construction of that of his son, Hon. Abiel Wood, a noted merchant, banker, shipowner and politician, who at one time represented the Lincoln District in Congress, was begun during the War of 1812, for the momentum of Wiscasset commerce carried part way through that disastrous time; but business reverses compelled suspension of work upon it for several years, as well as the elimination of some of the original specifications, and occupancy by the owner was not enjoyed until October, 1824. The house stands in a commanding location at the terminus of High Street and it is now occupied by descendants of the original owner. The houses of his brothers, Joseph Tinkham Wood and Hartley Wood, have also been preserved. The Joseph Tinkham Wood House, dating from 1805, was subjected to alteration in 1858, but certain of its most interesting features were fortunately retained and it is still notable for its stately entrance and its beautiful front hall and winding staircase. Wood's occupancy of it was cut short when he traded the house, and the land where it stands, to Moses Carlton, Jr., for a cargo of rum then recently landed on the latter's wharf in Wiscasset and valued at $12,000; and from Carlton's occupancy of fifty years it is more commonly known as the Carlton House. The Hartley Wood House, of less pretentious construction but still noteworthy in certain details, is now the summer home of the talented actress, Claire Eames.

We have seen that Wiscasset was incorporated in 1760. Its original corporate name was Pownalborough, it being thus called in honor of Thomas Pownall, who was then Governor of the Province of Massachusetts Bay, the jurisdiction of which extended over what is now the state of Maine. At about the time of the incorporation of Pownalborough a new county was established in these "Eastern parts," and Pownalborough was made the shire town, the courts of which were at first, and for several years, held in the western precinct adjacent to the Kennebec River. The advantages of Wiscasset harbor exceed those of that section around the Kennebec, and they were so rapidly availed of after the Revolutionary War closed that the growth of business and population at Wiscasset Point led to the removal of the courts hither—all unitedly attracting ambitious young men to locate here. The corporate name was soon afterward changed to Wiscasset.

And so came Silas Lee, a native of Concord, Massachusetts, who graduated at Harvard College in 1784. Establishing himself at Wiscasset, where he ever after resided, Lee's law practice increased apace. He also entered political life, and while a member of the Congress he resigned his post to accept an appointment by President Jefferson as United States Attorney for the District of Maine.

Early in the period of his residence here, Lee began to acquire real estate, and eventually secured several very desirable parcels, a part of which he developed with apparent profit. Of such lands he at first selected for a place of residence that through which High and Lee streets now run, and the first house that he put up was that in High Street which is now known as the Smith House. It is suggested that this house dates from 1792 for, although an earlier date has been assigned for its erection, it was not until that year that Lee cleared off a cloud upon the title, arising under the claims of the Wiscasset proprietors, to the land where it stands. It ranges on a line with the Abiel Wood House and the Carlton House on that side of High Street which, from an architectural point of view, has been called the most interesting in Maine. In his journal of travels in Maine in 1796 the Rev. Paul Coffin alluded to this house as "the noble edifice of Lawyer Lee." On the same tour he noticed that Wiscasset then had "eight or ten majestic houses, and many decent, and of a common two-story size."

Judge Lee sold his High Street house to Gen. David Payson in June, 1807. Shortly after the death of Gen. Payson, in 1831, the house passed into the hands of Samuel E. Smith, who at about that time was Governor of the state of Maine, and it is now the home of his descendants.

Judge Lee's manners and address were distinguished for suavity, and at their several houses he and Mrs. Lee were fond of entertaining the Justices of Supreme Judicial Court and other dignitaries and men of parts who visited Wiscasset, and pleasing traditions of their fragrant hospitality may yet be encountered.

Nearby the Smith House, and at the head of The Common, stands the Lincoln County Court House, the oldest building in Maine in which courts are now held. Its beautiful façade is notable for the perfect arches of its front windows and door. The date of its erection is shown by the simple but charming figures, 1824, which appear on the small, marble keystone in the arch at the entrance. This is the only one of the buildings here mentioned the cost of which is known, such cost being shown in the accounts of the agent for its construction as $10,843.09. Since May, 1825, terms of the Supreme Judicial Court have been held in this court house. Terms of United States courts have been held here; and at the bar have appeared the celebrated Jeremiah Mason, then of Boston, and many other distinguished lawyers, including Daniel Webster, "then," as one of his associates afterwards wrote, "in the full flush of his success and in the zenith of his power as a master of eloquence."

Looking at the spruce frame of a building erected in Wiscasset in 1872, William Chick, of many years' experience in house building, remarked: "Well, spruce is good lumber, but white pine is good enough for me." It was he who kept for many years a few well seasoned white-pine planks so that when his end should come, good white pine lumber would be available for a watertight box to hold his coffin.

COURT HOUSE, WISCASSET, MAINE

ABIEL WOOD HOUSE, WISCASSET, MAINE

NICKELS-SORTWELL HOUSE—1807-1808—WISCASSET, MAINE

Detail of Main Façade
NICKELS-SORTWELL HOUSE, WISCASSET, MAINE

Detail of Entrance Hall
NICKELS-SORTWELL HOUSE, WISCASSET, MAINE

Stairway Detail
NICKELS-SORTWELL HOUSE, WISCASSET, MAINE

General View
LEE-SMITH HOUSE, WISCASSET, MAINE

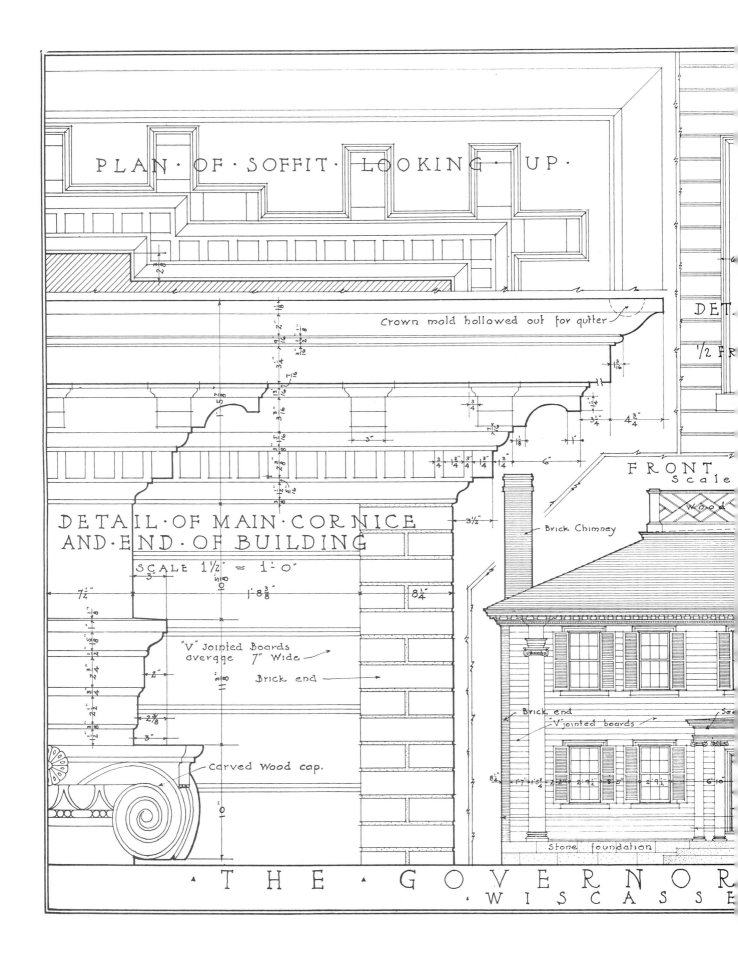

PLAN · OF · SOFFIT · LOOKING · UP ·

Crown mold hollowed out for gutter

DET.

½ FR

FRONT

Scale

DETAIL · OF · MAIN · CORNICE
AND · END · OF BUILDING

SCALE 1½" = 1'-0"

"V" Jointed Boards
average 7" Wide

Brick end

Carved wood cap.

Brick Chimney

Wood

Brick end
"V jointed boards

See

Stone foundation

· THE · GOVERNOR
· WISCASSE

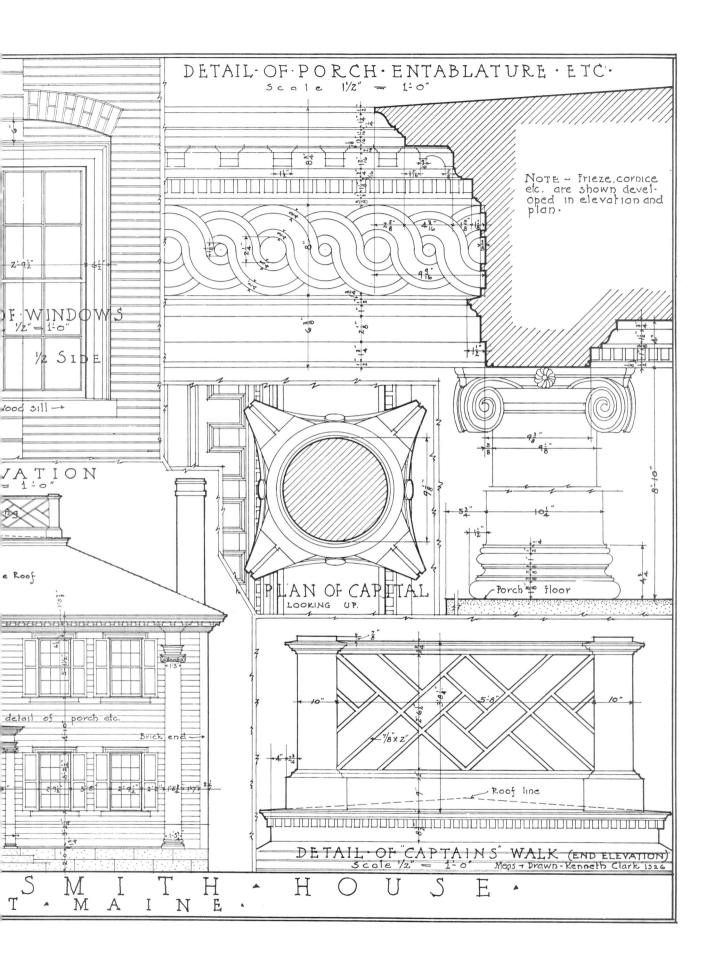

DETAIL·OF·PORCH·ENTABLATURE·ETC·
Scale 1½" = 1'-0"

NOTE ~ Frieze, cornice
etc. are shown devel-
oped in elevation and
plan.

OF·WINDOWS
½" = 1'-0"

½ SIDE

wood sill →

VATION
= 1'-0"

e Roof

detail of porch etc.

Brick end →

PLAN OF CAPITAL
LOOKING UP.

Porch floor

Roof line

7/8" x 2"

DETAIL·OF·"CAPTAINS"·WALK (END ELEVATION)
Scale ½" = 1'-0"   Meas + Drawn ~ Kenneth Clark 1926

SMITH · HOUSE ·
T · MAINE ·

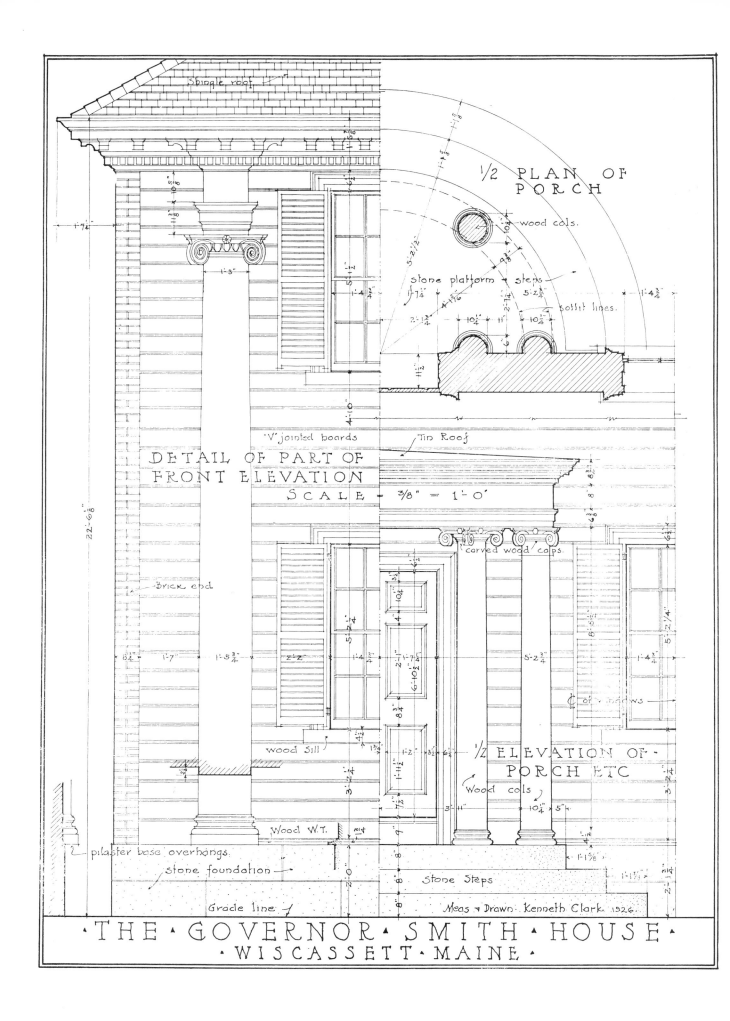

Shingle roof

½ PLAN OF
PORCH

wood cols.

stone platform   steps

soffit lines.

"V' jointed boards   Tin Roof

DETAIL OF PART OF
FRONT ELEVATION
SCALE = 3/8" = 1'-0'

carved wood cols.

Brick end

₵ of windows

Wood Sill

½ ELEVATION OF
PORCH ETC

Wood cols

pilaster base overhangs.

stone foundation

Wood W.T.

Stone Steps

Grade line

Meas & Drawn. Kenneth Clark. 1926.

·THE·GOVERNOR·SMITH·HOUSE·
·WISCASSETT·MAINE·

Detail of Front Porch
LEE-SMITH HOUSE, WISCASSET, MAINE

Detail of Front Porch
LEE-SMITH HOUSE, WISCASSET, MAINE

LEE-SMITH HOUSE — c1792 — WISCASSET, MAINE
Now known as the Governor S. E. Smith House

AMES HOUSE, WISCASSET, MAINE

HOUSE OVERLOOKING THE HARBOR, WISCASSET, MAINE

Double-Hung Window
GOV. SMITH HOUSE, WISCASSET, MAINE

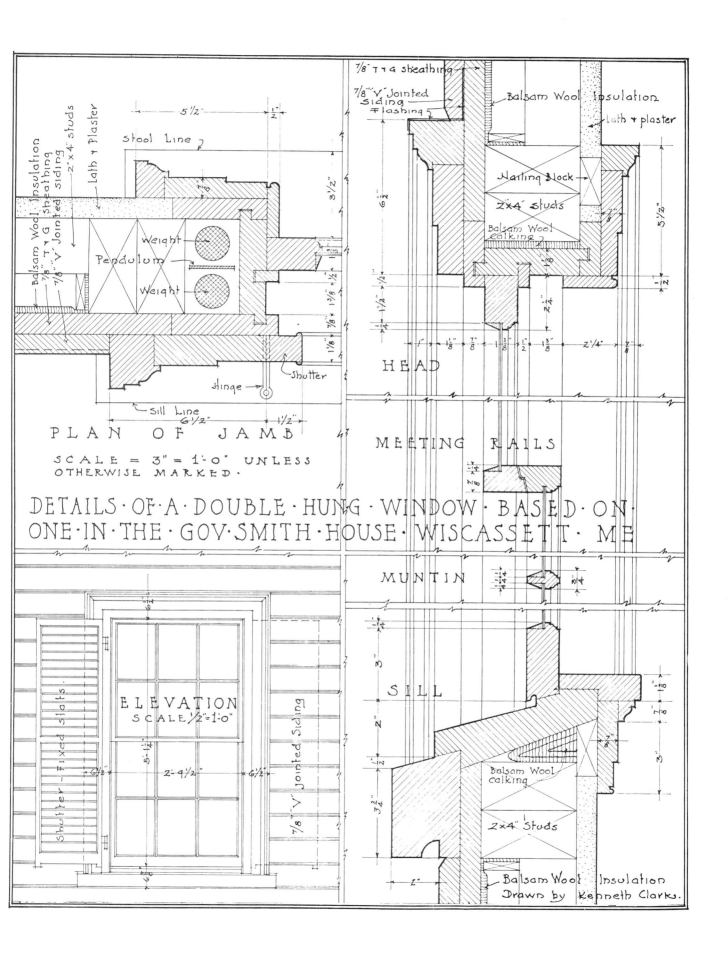

DETAILS·OF·A·DOUBLE·HUNG·WINDOW·BASED·ON·
ONE·IN·THE·GOV·SMITH·HOUSE·WISCASSETT·ME

PLAN OF JAMB

SCALE = 3"= 1'·0" UNLESS
OTHERWISE MARKED.

ELEVATION
SCALE ½"= 1'·0"

HEAD

MEETING RAILS

MUNTIN

SILL

Drawn by Kenneth Clark.

CLAPP HOUSE, WISCASSET, MAINE

Dependencies of the
Old-Fashioned House

Text by
Irving B. Eventworth
Originally published in 1922 as White Pine Monograph
Volume VIII, Number 2

Barn and Woodshed
CAPTAIN ABRAHAM BURBANK HOUSE — c1790 — SUFFIELD, CONNECTICUT

DEPENDENCIES OF THE OLD-FASHIONED HOUSE

LIVING in the country a hundred years or more ago was by no means the simple matter that it is today. The farmer generally raised most of his own living on his own farm; he didn't buy it from the corner grocery store, and in consequence he needed a number of small buildings for storage and for the simple manufacturing processes of the farm which have now become obsolete. Nowadays practically the only dependencies on the small country place are the garage and such ornamental structures as may be needed to accentuate the features of the garden. Formerly the well equipped small farm had an extensive stable, cow barns, carriage house, sheds for tools and vehicles, a smokehouse, a summer kitchen, corn-cribs, summerhouses, chicken coops, well-heads, and another type of structure which I can best describe by telling how some elderly aunts of mine in re-modeling an old farmhouse (being delicately minded) talked to the contractor of the "cabinet": when he made his drawings they were much surprised to find "cabin B" out in the back yard.

The quality and design of all these dependencies naturally varied very greatly with the means and tastes of the owners, but it is not infrequent to find small outbuildings in which the design is quite as careful as that of the house, and in complete conformity to its style. This was especially true of those outbuildings which were erected in the immediate vicinity of the house and were intimately related to the activities of the house. Stables for the owner's driving horses, for example, were usually placed near the house, often connected to it, especially in the northern part of New England, and were treated in much the same style as that of the house, although with a less degree of ornament.

A curious feature of these dependencies in colonial times was that their design showed a surprising lack of adaptation to their purposes and little expression of the uses of the buildings. Certain features, notably the well-heads and summerhouses in the garden, were of such shapes and of such requirements that it was impossible, or at least difficult, to reproduce miniature houses. A trellised arbor, for example, in a garden is necessarily open to the breezes on all sides, and must afford a support for vines in order that it may properly fulfill its function. Summerhouses, therefore, have compelled the designers to display originality and ingenuity beyond the point they reached in many of the other buildings. Even in these garden-houses there is a tendency to reproduce buildings or portions of buildings in miniature. This is not surprising if one stops to consider the methods of design in colonial times. The architect as we know him today was practically non-existent, and for the most part the delightful colonial houses were not drawn at all, but were just built, with the ornamental features such as doorways, cornices, windows, porches, etc., copied out of one of the books then in use, such as *Palladio Londinienses* or, later, Asher Benjamin's *Country Carpenter's Assistant*. The men who were doing these houses had learned their mass proportion by experiment, the size of their windows was determined by available glass sizes, and all ornament copied, so that they probably used drawing instruments with difficulty, or not at all; and nobody can design without a pencil. Therefore, when they were forced to build garden structures of small size and without precedent or available designs, they copied either a small portion of some design at hand or reduced the scale of the book design to the required size. A notable example is the gazebo of the Royall House at Medford, Massachusetts, which was nothing but the crowning member of a church spire or the cupola of a public building set upon a raised mound. It is extremely entertaining, but one unquestionably has the feeling that the building upon which it rests has disappeared into the earth through some cataclysm of nature, and one would expect to be able to excavate a buried Pompeii or a New England city of Ys from the ground below. One of these garden structures which is doubtless perfectly familiar to every architect is the tea-house of the Derby estate. Naturally a little building so amusing and so characteristically Colonial as this would not escape frequent publication, but since its design illustrates so well the point I want to make, I cannot refrain from mentioning it in this sketch. The first floor of the building was intended for the storage of tools, and the second floor for a summerhouse or tea-house, but the design is really that of a public building for a colony of dolls rather than of a garden structure pure and simple.

Toward the end of the colonial period our ancestors began using little models of Greek temples for houses, and obsessed with the idea that one must have a Greek temple or nothing, they built even their dependencies in this characteristic fashion. The

Gazebo
ROYALL HOUSE, MEDFORD, MASSACHUSETTS

ELIAS H. DERBY TEA-HOUSE,
PEABODY, MASSACHUSETTS

springhouse of the Goodloe Harper House, near Baltimore, Maryland, is a most excellent example; and on the North Country Road near Massapequa, Long Island, there is a very pleasant Greek temple house with a sort of baby temple alongside, the baby temple having been used as an office for the owner of the estate. It is curious among early architects, as illustrated in this Massapequa house, to find that a considerable alteration of scale apparently troubled the designer not at all. What he was after was a similar design regardless of the scale, and very frequently we find cases of similar treatment of different sizes of buildings. The barn of Vesper Cliff, at Owego, New York, might be taken for a small church if one didn't know that it was used for a barn, but on the other hand the barn of the Burbank House, at Suffield, Connecticut, has been designed with large entrances, is in scale with the house, and is a mighty attractive building as well. Designs such as this were the exception rather than the rule with the early architects; at least I have seen comparatively few examples either in reality or in photographs; which probably accounts for the familiarity of the few remaining examples, such as the stable of the Pierce-

Springhouse and Dairy
ESTATE OF GOODLOE HARPER — c1800 — BALTIMORE COUNTY, MARYLAND

Barn
VESPER CLIFF (JOHNSON-PLATT HOUSE) — c1830 — OWEGO, NEW YORK

Nichols House, at Salem, a very pleasant piece of architecture, and very distinctly a stable, although quite at one in character with the house to which it is attached. A similar instance will occur to the members of the American Institute of Architects in the stable of the Octagon, at Washington.

The stable of the Pierce-Nichols House is the only country example which occurs to me of the common European stable form, in which the stable was built around a central court, and there existed even in the cities comparatively few examples of this pleasant form of construction.

Detail of "Cabin B"
ROCKWELL HOUSE, WINSTED, CONNECTICUT

Its origin was doubtless due to the medieval necessity for protection against enemies, but our climate is quite as great an enemy as a band of robbers, and one which is always with us, so it is surprising to find so few instances of large stable groups planned in this logical and traditional fashion. Its obvious advantages of the protection against wind and snow would seem sufficient so that our colonial ancestors, with their many horses and cattle, would have selected it for much country work, instead of planning their farm buildings in a row, as was usually the

Dependencies
ANDREW B. HARRING HOUSE, NORTHVALE, NEW JERSEY

Barn

CAPTAIN ABRAHAM BURBANK HOUSE—c1790—SUFFIELD, CONNECTICUT

Dependencies

ROCKWELL HOUSE — 1813 — WINSTED, CONNECTICUT

Dependencies
BACON HOUSE, KENT, CONNECTICUT

perhaps of all these examples is that at Winsted, Connecticut, where a little group, consisting of the carriage house and "cabin B," was built at the rear of the farmhouse, the farmhouse cornice being followed at the same scale on the carriage house, and same design duplicated at a reduced scale carried on pigmy pilasters on the "cabin."

There was a certain class of dependencies which has not been previously mentioned but which had a real bearing on modern architecture, and that is the slave quarters, common throughout the South and even fairly frequent in the Middle States and New England. I imagine that most Northern people and many Southern people do not realize that the last slaves held in the United States were in the state of Delaware in 1867, and that slavery in Connecticut was not abolished until some years after the Revolution. These slave quarters were, especially in the northern states, often of substantial and attractive construction, suitable for precedent for the small country cottages of today, and a sort of natural ancestor of

case. Nor was its size alone sufficient to cause its relinquishment; most farms needed sufficient buildings to enclose a court, and my only explanation is that the colonial farm groups were in most cases aggregations of buildings erected when necessity impelled, rather than designed or even mentally provided for in advance by the owners.

In buildings of the farmhouse type it was very common to place certain dependencies in a wing of the building or in a separate structure attached to the main building by a covered passageway. Many of the quaintest and most attractive old Dutch farmhouses were treated in this manner, the Andrew B. Harring House, at Northvale, New Jersey, being a typical Middle States example, partially of stone and partially of wood; while the Bacon House, at Kent, Connecticut, is typical of New England. It may be said in general that the farther north one goes the more frequently these dependencies were connected to the house by an interior passage, and what was occasional in Connecticut became customary in New Hampshire and Vermont. One of the most amusing

Court Yard
PIERCE-NICHOLS HOUSE, SALEM, MASSACHUSETTS

the superintendent's or gardener's cottage of large estates. The example illustrated at Woodbury, Connecticut, is now used as a tea-house, and is interesting as showing not only the house itself but also an amusing example of a well covering, although the well covering has no claims to architectural merit. I am sorry to see the old well-head disappear, although I am glad that our drinking water no longer comes from the wells; but such a one as that of East Greenwich, Rhode Island, illustrated on page 222, is an extremely picturesque feature of the country place, and one which we are, alas, no longer called upon to design. The colonial designer of this well-head was able to free himself from the desire to duplicate in miniature the motives of the house. The building is of course not much bigger in size than the largest piece of colonial furniture, and in design the designer has considered furniture precedent rather than outdoor construction. The cornice resembles the cornice of the old kitchen cabinets or of corner cupboards rather than that of a house, and is,

Stable and Woodshed
HOUSE AT PORTSMOUTH, NEW HAMPSHIRE

of course, much better adapted in scale and in profile to act as a crowning mass than would be the typical classic cornice. The well-head in this country never reached the interest and beauty of many of the European examples, in which masonry and wrought iron work were so freely employed, but our old well-heads did have a quality of their own, and the fact that they were constructed of wood painted white, very often with green louvers, gave one a feeling that the water within was pure, cool, and sparkling, such as no nickel-plated faucet or white lavatory can inspire. It is too bad that the old quaint customs were so often inconvenient or unsanitary, and that as most well-heads covered dug wells of little depth the water was often apt to be polluted from the drainage of the house.

Of the many charming examples of garden architecture left to us from colonial times it seems unnecessary to speak at length. There was a surprising similarity in their design from Maine to South Carolina. The use of trellised arches for roses and other climbing vines was a common feature to mark the entrance to the gar-

Old Slave Quarters
BACON HOUSE, WOODBURY, CONNECTICUT

den. The turns of the paths were very frequently covered by summerhouses of square or octagonal shape, with ingenious variations in the trellis and treatment of the hoods. These were sometimes open and trellised, sometimes closed and shingled, and in some cases portions of the roof were left open while the center part was covered. They became almost automatically a feature of every colonial garden; sometimes only a place on which flowers or grapes could be grown and sometimes a genuine gazebo, but always the interest of the

Outhouse
FORT JOHNSON HOUSE, AMSTERDAM, NEW YORK

gardens of which they formed a part was greatly enhanced by their white-painted or whitewashed outlines gleaming through the shrubbery and flowers. They are the best evidences, I think, that our ancestors were able to design in a more or less playful spirit and that the dour New England conscience was unable to resist the pleasure and brightness of its gardens. New Englanders were flower lovers, if we ever had flower lovers, and it is a pleasant thing to remember, especially in these days when the New England con-

Stable and West Approach
DE WOLF-MIDDLETON HOUSE, PAPASQUE NECK, BRISTOL, RHODE ISLAND

SUMMERHOUSE AT NEWBURYPORT, MASSACHUSETTS

purity and refinement of composition together with great ingenuity in making slight fundamental variations of design.

When one considers the variety of uses to which the dependencies of colonial buildings were put, one is surprised to find their design so generally similar to that of the dwelling-house. It would seem that the very factors which made for the extraordinarily high quality of taste in ornament and of correctness in mass in colonial work tended to confine the imagination of the colonial designers. It is well to remember that architectural design is necessarily limited within rather narrow bounds by the limitations of tradition and precedent; that in colonial days there were few precedents; and that the knowledge of precedent, other than Classic, was practically none. So, in judging the work of the early American designers we must realize that their minds ran in narrow but exceedingly deep grooves of tradition, and we should not be surprised that their work was so uniform, either in the type of design or in its quality. We are accustomed to attribute to these early American designers a greater average ability than they possessed, because their work was so consistently excellent.

science has become a thing to be ashamed of rather than admired.

One dependency of the colonial house I do not find among this collection of illustrations, the grape arbor. Our colonial ancestors not only liked flowers, but also, I am pleased rather than regretful to say, liked the pressed juice of the grape after it had been kept for a while and put in casks or bottles; so to the Italian pergola precedent we have added the American grape arbor as a boundary motive to our estates or gardens.

As in Colonial work in general, we find a rather narrow range of architecture in the

Old Terraced Garden, Back of the Barn
PIERCE-NICHOLS HOUSE, SALEM, MASSACHUSETTS

dependencies of the colonial houses. I always think of Greek and Colonial architecture as having in common that both styles were perfected within narrow limits, set possibly by their ignorance of many precedents, possibly by the purity of their tastes. As the colonial builders and the Greeks alike were compelled to use ornament sparingly, its use became quite an event, and its design and execution were thoroughly studied. Again the architecture of both periods depends upon the masses of the structures and the refinement and position of their moldings rather than upn elaborate composition or complicated detail; so we find in colonial as in Greek a

Summerhouse
ENDICOTT GARDEN, DANVERS, MASSACHUSETTS

Well-Head
EAST GREENWICH, RHODE ISLAND

Fences and Fenceposts

Text by
Alfred Hopkins
Originally published in 1922 as White Pine Monograph
Volume VIII, Number 6

Urn and Fencepost
PIERCE-NICHOLS HOUSE—1782—SALEM, MASSACHUSETTS
Samuel McIntire, Architect

FENCES AND FENCEPOSTS
OF COLONIAL TIMES

WHEN Mr. Whitehead asked me to write an article on old picket fences for the very interesting and instructive series on Colonial architecture, I accepted the task with alacrity, because it gave me an opportunity of venting in public print a view which I have frequently had to repress in private, that of all the various problems submitted by the layman to the architect for his suggestion, the subject of the fence, as it is generally presented, is the most inane and uninteresting. Every architect, I take it, can recall the incident of the smiling and vain-glorious purchaser of a piece of country real estate breezing into his office, and, with a self-sufficient air, saying that he has secured a wonderful site, that he wants to do the perfect piece of architecture, some-day — but not now — and that he is very anxious to discuss just what type of fence ought to be put up in the interim. It is then that I wish breezy people would not think about fences, and would permit me to occupy my

mind with thoughts which better please my fancy.

But, in looking over the editor's delightful collection of photographs of early American fences and fenceposts, many of which have been selected to illustrate this chapter, it is very easy to be led into a discussion of them, and a first impulse is to incline one to the opinion that all the possible forms for the American fence have been devised, and that it is only the province of the present day architect to make a judicious selection; this certainly is the view evidenced by the most casual student of furniture design. We do not have time in our hurried life to take pains with the little things, and that is the principal reason why so much of our modern architecture is crude and ill-considered.

There is perhaps not so much to learn from European countries with respect to fence design as there is from our own colonial period, which was rich in this particular. England has given us excellent exam-

Fence and Gateway
HOUSE AT LAUREL, LONG ISLAND

CHESTNUT STREET LOOKING WEST, SALEM, MASSACHUSETTS

The tall solid masonry walls of the Continental estate are not friendly in America, nor are they desirable or necessary here, where we have endless land and comparatively little population. The impulse for privacy on the part of the well-to-do is just as insistent today as ever, or the owner of a newly bought piece of property would not rush into an architect's office and ask for something arresting in the way of fence design. In crowded Europe, however, the solid wall was frequently the only thing which gave privacy, but for America I have always felt, that, as a general principle, a fence which was not absolutely necessary had better be done away with altogether, although, if the conditions actually required such protection, it should not obstruct the landscape, but rather give the passerby as extended a view of Nature's loveliness as is possible. It is astonishing, where, in a rocky country, the farmers have laid the stones into many fences, how much these barriers interfere with the view of the

Fence Detail
HOUSE IN NEWBURYPORT, MASSACHUSETTS

ples of the ambitious iron fence, but it has had no very great development here. In rare instances, our architects have designed fine iron fences, but more often they have failed, and the usual flamboyant structure of this variety serves only to enclose the palace of a billionaire, a building usually so turbulent and ill at ease in architectural outline, that one feels it might somehow, wriggle out of its environment, unless the site was securely enclosed in an iron construction.

Once upon a time, when our ancestors spoke of their "defences," they referred to the great walls and battlements which protected them against their warlike neighbors; but, nowadays our neighbors are among neighborly, and the "defences" have dwindled down to "fences." The evolution of the fence has proceeded in accordance with the nature of the marauders to be shut out; the utmost that is required of a fence in this day and country is a stout resistance to little boys, cows or chickens.

Fence Detail
HOUSE IN NEWBURYPORT, MASSACHUSETTS

landscape. To prove the statement, it is necessary only to take down these crisscross scars on the green-sward, as the author has done many times, to see how the view is opened up thereby, and how the land leaps out in acreage before you. Even on an estate's outside edge, I have always resented the intrusion of a high stone fence as being unfriendly and un-neighborly, and usually, I find, that it is better manners and better architecture to do away with such unsightly obstructions. The traveler in Spain will see the gigantic cactus frequently planted in rows as a

FENCEPOST—NEWBURYPORT, MASSACHUSETTS

fence, and it makes a decidedly effective barrier. We have varieties of thorns which will do equally well and in fact the whole idea of using planting as a means of designating boundaries or creating barriers is an ingratiating one, and we hope our *confrères*, the landscape architects, may take it up and develop it. As for ourselves, we have not been very much encouraged by the way the suggestion has been received by the laity. Iron, stone or wood as a material are what drift into the mind of the average man when he is inspired by the thought that the time has come when he

FENCE AND FENCEPOSTS—NEWBURYPORT, MASSACHUSETTS

must begin to build fences.

All this, however, has to do with present day problems, in the great American republic in the year of our Lord, 1922. Let us proceed to a less fatiguing prospect and try to adjust our imaginations to how engaging life may have been in the pleasant town of Salem, as depicted by the photograph of Chestnut Street. Here we have fence design in its most beautiful and appropriate flowering. Here are privacy and a proper regard for one's neighbors, expressed in faultless fashion.

What is true of Chestnut Street,

FENCEPOST—NEWBURYPORT, MASSACHUSETTS

Salem, is also true of High Street in Newburyport. In both of these Massachusetts towns the fence is often an integral part of the approach, an introduction, as it were, to the motifs to be found in the decoration of the porches and of the house itself.

Nothing could be better architecture than the types of fence and fenceposts shown in the illustrations on pages 227, 228, and 229. What could be more in keeping than the old house and the fence at Laurel, Long Island, illustrated on page 225, though the gateposts have a strong suspicion of the influence of the Vic-

Fence

HAVEN HOUSE, PORTSMOUTH, NEW HAMPSHIRE

JUDGE HAYES' HOUSE AND FENCE, SOUTH BERWICK, MAINE

Fence and Fenceposts
WENTWORTH HOUSE, PORTSMOUTH, NEW HAMPSHIRE

328 ESSEX STREET, SALEM, MASSACHUSETTS

HOUSE ON OUTSKIRTS OF BOSTON, MASSACHUSETTS

TWO FENCES AND FENCEPOSTS OF COLONIAL TIMES

torian era? This is the simplest type of fence conceivable, but it is good American architecture, nevertheless, and we cannot help calling attention to Nature's most delightful bit of architecture, shown in the branches of the old apple tree in the foreground.

For a perfect example of a Colonial fence, we call attention to the illustration on the upper half of page 232 and the upper right-hand corner of page 235, showing the fence in front of the

possible; at any rate, here is an old-time essay which well illustrates the general principles enunciated above. The horizontal rails of the fence have been moulded, to lighten their effect, and the base has been kept low. The detail of the post is delicate and refined, and the urn on the top is perhaps the only feature which needs to be reduced in the scale of its ornamentation, but that only very slightly.

A type of fence which is both effective and al-

Gateposts and Gate

H. K. OLIVER HOUSE—c1799—SALEM, MASSACHUSETTS

The urns and gateposts were originally part of the palatial home constructed by the mariner, Elias H. Derby.

Loring-Emmerton House, at 328 Essex Street, Salem, Massachusetts. The pickets are exactly right in size, and it is easy for the architect to imagine how much heavier they would be had they been left to modern draughting room methods of detailing. The whole design is of absorbing interest in showing how every part has been treated to conform to the designer's feeling for lightness and grace. Perhaps his thought was to obstruct the view of the landscape as little as

ways satisfactory for use as a street boundary is the one on High Street, Newburyport, Massachusetts, shown at the bottom of page 227. Its design is frequently repeated in present day fences, but often the fine proportions of the old-time one are lost, because the modern tendency is to make it all too heavy.

In the old fence in front of the Wentworth House, Portsmouth, illustrated on page 231, is seen such a pleasant combination of the open and the closed fence, that in regard to the solid portion, we are quite willing to withdraw what we have written about obscuring the landscape and being unneighborly. Let us hope that something unseemly is kept from the public view, in which case we can stick to our principles, without being embarrassed by having to admit an exception.

The gateway, shown on page 238, of the Admiral Cowles House, at Farmington, Connecticut, built about 1790, is very effectively and unusually well designed and would lend itself

the corners, between which is a semicircular fencing, with the smaller gateposts between them. In the present instance, however, the urns, while generally in keeping, may possibly be revised copies of excellent originals.

The fence shown on page 230 of Judge Hayes' House, South Berwick, Maine, is effective in that it accentuates the posts by keeping the fencing between them very light. The elevated position of the house on the terrace, the garden spot to the right, are all very attractive and very

Gateway and Fence
HOME OF JAMES RUSSELL LOWELL, CAMBRIDGE, MASSACHUSETTS

particularly well to garden gate design, rather than as precedent for a main entrance gate; although here it serves its aesthetic and practical purpose well.

At Stamford, Connecticut, and at Vergennes, Vermont, we have fencing which is more similar to modern methods of design, and the increased weight of the parts is not to its advantage, though the fenceposts are well done.

In the picture of the fence and gateway of the "King" Caesar House, at Duxbury, Massachusetts, is shown a simple, usual and effective way of accentuating the entrance, by main posts at

typical of the hill country, and the house shown is a distinctive example of architecture and planting as exemplified in the American home.

We are happy to draw to a conclusion in the contemplation of so much good taste as was shown by the early craftsman who built this house in Maine, and we do so with an earnest appeal to those interested in early American architecture — white pine architecture, if you will — for it was that — to study this illustration well. Here is the perfect piece of architecture which our vainglorious friend is going to build on his newly acquired parcel of real estate, but never does,

FENCEPOSTS AND URNS — SALEM AND NEWBURYPORT

Fence
LEWIS HOUSE, BROOKFIELD, MASSACHUSETTS

Fence and Gateway
"KING" CAESAR HOUSE, DUXBURY, MASSACHUSETTS

Gateway
SMITH HOUSE, VERGENNES, VERMONT

One can see how it would be possible to reconstruct from the documents that are furnished us by the matter under consideration at this time an history of all the salient characteristics of colonial design; just as it is possible for the anthropologist to reconstruct from a few scattered fragments of the skeleton of some prehistoric animal, a complete and accurate model of every detail of that animal's appearance.

If we, as I have said, do not have time in our hurried life to take pains with little things, the colonial designer, fortunately, had the necessary time and, what is even better, the determination and inclination to do his best in even the smallest and most inconsiderable details in connection with the work at which he was engaged.

If one were placed as Michelangelo was during the building of St. Peter's at Rome, and could say to his client as Michelangelo did to the Cardinals who were determined to dictate to him in matters of design that "your duty, Gentlemen," — or as the architect would say to his twentieth century client, "your duty sir," — "is to furnish me with the money to pay for the building; and my duty is to design that building," many things might be more popularly and more successfully managed.

Someone has suggested that we may follow the entire economic history of American agriculture in

and I will venture the statement, as a fact, that this owner did not commence his homebuilding by surrounding the vacant property with the finely designed fence which has called forth our approbation!

No — by no means did the colonial architect do his work in that back-handed manner. The fence that surrounded the house or at least that shut it off from too direct contact with every casual passerby on the street must have been more than a mere inconsequential detail to him.

It must have been, I have always felt, quite as important a part of the entire design as the entrance doorway, the interior paneling or the exquisitely designed window frames that the colonial architect used whenever the opportunity presented itself.

Indeed it seems that there is hardly space in one number of this series to discuss to any satisfactory extent the total possibilities of the "Fences and Fenceposts of Colonial Times."

As a matter of fact, there would be no great risk in suggesting that the entire development of Colonial architecture unfolds itself to a large extent in matters even so small as the general attitude of the designer to the slightest detail connected with the Colonial fence.

Gateway
HOUSE NEAR STAMFORD, CONNECTICUT

the fences that surround the American farm, just as I have suggested, that we may follow the history of American architecture in the fenceposts of colonial times. For is it not true that such primitive and economical fences as that in the house at Laurel, Long Island, are quite as typical of the general process of thought of the back woods farmer as are the splendidly designed gate posts of the Oliver House in Salem, a typical example of what the conscientious architect would wish to produce, even under the most unsatisfactory conditions, and which fortunately he can produce on those happy occasions when the right conditions present themselves?

One thing at least is illustrated by the examples shown in this chapter, and that is the happy faculty possessed by the colonial architect of breaking up the monotony of his work by a few well chosen spots of ornament. The illustrations show us, too, how the colonial architect heeded the admonition of an early writer on architecture who in the middle of the seventeenth century expressed the warning to his readers, "to use, and still be sparing of antik ornaments."

Entrance Gateway
ADMIRAL COWLES HOUSE, FARMINGTON, CONNECTICUT

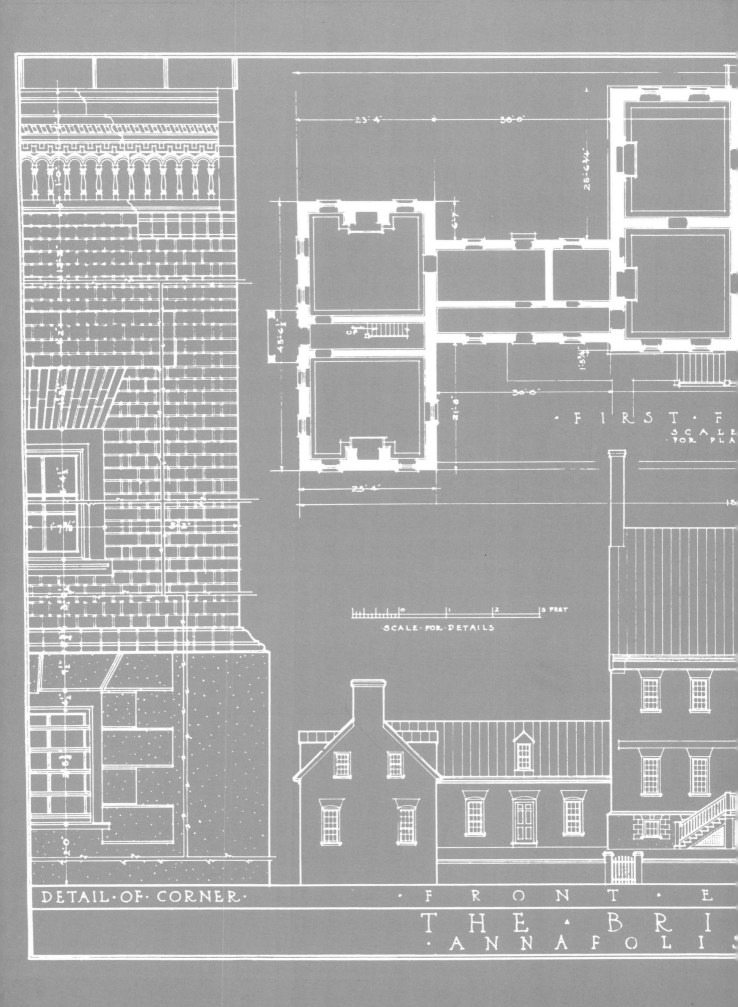

23' 4"   30'-0"

26'-6¼"

45'-6"

30'-0"

23' 4"

· F I R S T · F
SCAL
FOR · PLA

|0 | | 2 | 3 FEET
SCALE · FOR · DETAILS

DETAIL · OF · CORNER ·   · F R O N T · E
T H E · B R I
· A N N A P O L I S